Clinical
Psycholinguistics

COGNITION AND LANGUAGE
A Series in Psycholinguistics

Series Editor: **R. W. Rieber**

CLINICAL PSYCHOLINGUISTICS
Theodore Shapiro

CRAZY TALK: A Study of the Discourse of Schizophrenic Speakers
Sherry Rochester and J. R. Martin

PSYCHOLOGY OF LANGUAGE AND LEARNING
O. Hobart Mowrer

A Continuation Order Plan is available for this series. A continuation order will bring delivery of each new volume immediately upon publication. Volumes are billed only upon actual shipment. For further information please contact the publisher.

Clinical
Psycholinguistics

Theodore Shapiro

Cornell University Medical College
New York, New York

Plenum Press · New York and London

Library of Congress Cataloging in Publication Data

Shapiro, Theodore.
 Clinical psycholinguistics.

 (Cognition and language)
 Includes index.
 1. Psychotherapy. 2. Psycholinguistics. I. Title. II. Series.
 RC480.5.S444   616.8'9'0019   79-22018
 ISBN 0-306-40249-1

© 1979 Plenum Press, New York
A Division of Plenum Publishing Corporation
227 West 17th Street, New York, N.Y. 10011

Printed in the United States of America

To Joan, Susan, and Zander

Acknowledgments

This volume grows out of many experiences with so many colleagues and patients who cannot be named but to whom I offer thanks. Dr. Victor Rosen, now deceased, provided the direction and early guidance. My family encouraged me and was patient. Without Esther Lewis, the manuscript would have remained only a thought.

Contents

Introduction

One of Molière's gauche characters in *Le Bourgeoise Gentilhomme* responds with surprise when he learns that he has been speaking prose all his life. The apparent discovery, reflected in his comment, provides us with both the virtues and the difficulties in presenting "yet another book," especially one with a somewhat ambitious title as this one. The virtues may be cataloged under cross-fertilization among a number of disciplines which provides impetus to new ideas, work, and even discoveries. The difficulties pertain to the difference in focus of each discipline, the difference in the object each discipline chooses to study, and the difference in specialized language that accrues between fields of inquiry.

Not too many years ago, natural science and especially psychology were within the confines of philosophy and its subsectors: the pre-Socratic philosophers were essentially cosmologists, and only later, with Socrates and Plato's work, did an interest in epistemology assume a central position within philosophy. Although this event put man at the center of philosophical inquiry, the emergence of techniques to study psychological processes *per se* was indeed late and, at that, long after natural science had edged away from philosophy. Recently, it is sometimes difficult to distinguish linguistics from philosophy, because there is a strong wave of philosophical thinking that is dependent on linguistic analysis, and the specialized linguistics of that area depends heavily on philosophical musings. Wittgenstein's admonition that we must be silent about that which we cannot say is perhaps the most concise statement about the central position of language within philosophy. While these trends in philosophy were emerging in some quarters, psychologists were constructing stimulus–response curves, establishing laws of learning, whereas others were involved in perceptual and cognitive studies.

Clinical psychologists and psychiatrists studied personality and psycho-pathology. Those psychologists who were not seduced to animal models seemed highly dependent on verbal responses and what these repre-sented in the realm of ideas. In this latter sense, therefore, human psy-chology focused considerably on verbal behavior.

If an unexamined life is not worth living, an unexamined faculty, such as language capacity, requires systematic questioning as well. It is in this spirit that a number of psychologists began using the models of linguistics and philosophy and a number of linguists became interested in the relationship between their understanding of language structure and mental organization. Thus, a hybrid science of *psycholinguistics* emerged. We are witnessing a new version of the Aristophanic myth, a paraphrase of which states, in the beginning, we were all united in a perfect androgyny, and it is only natural that men and women so segre-gated should again seek out each other in copulation to conceive and create a new product. Psycholinguistics, then, is not so strange an off-spring if we retain some awareness of its earlier union in philosophy.

However, the title of this book is *Clinical Psycholinguistics*, which suggests the possible intrusion of yet another "bedfellow" in an already hybrid science. Surely, we cannot morally justify a *ménage à trois* re-flected in the tripartite title. The justification must come from the en-richment suggested earlier that accrues from cross-fertilization among varying frames of reference and among a variety of scientific disciplines.

Even though, as author of this volume, I claim little faith in interdis-ciplinary colloquia *per se*, I have had the experience of hearing people of different disciplines speak clearly about what they do and present the models they work from, and this has provided a new stimulation that enriches my own practice. Some practicing psychotherapists suggest that the best path is to read the linguists and the psychologists them-selves and then to make one's own synthesis. I can only commend such an approach to knowledge. However, time does not permit most clinicians to study these alien areas, because time, like money, has a way of being squandered or utilized in those directions which an individual finds most pleasurable. Furthermore, I hope that, after a reading of this volume, additional and finer study might be contemplated.

There is yet another reason to consider this volume a virtue. If the reader will pardon an example from my own experience, I would like to mention a change in perspective in my own education. Having studied philosophy and especially the philosophy of science during my under-graduate years, I was especially excited when I learned that a gifted and scholarly physicist-philosopher I knew was to offer a brief course in the philosophy of science for medical students as part of their first-year curriculum at a new medical school. It took two years for this course to be included in the curriculum, and then it was only presented as a guest lectureship in five sessions. At that time, I had been in medical school for more than two years and eagerly attended the lectures of my former professor at the sister school. I experienced a striking sense which can only be characterized as "You can't go home again." Although much of what he included in his lectures had been familiar—having known the professor and his manner of thinking and presentation on prior occasions—the content was, by this time, alien and overabstract for what I was doing as a medical student. The examples were no longer relevant; they were not medical. The problems that needed to be solved through this philosophical discourse no longer seemed to apply to my current concerns, and I soon became aware that the relevance of this sort of a course could be brought home to students much more clearly by somebody who was knowledgeable in both fields. With this apology presented and the self-justification made public, I would like, at the outset, to introduce myself as a clinician who, in the course of an academic and professional career, has had the opportunity to study linguistics and psychology because they converged in an area of work which, early in my research, commanded my interest. Moreover, I have had the opportunity, along with other colleagues who were similarly interested in language study, to attend a seminar originally run by Dr. Victor Rosen at the New York Psychoanalytic Institute. There we not only had visiting lecturers in linguistics but also began to apply some of our learning to clinical practice. We hoped our new knowledge might help us reorganize some of our thinking within the clinical psychoanalytic idiom. We looked to this particular area of knowledge because it does not permit a reductionism to physiology or to chemistry. Rather it is a discipline with mentalist propositions, and it offers clinicians who are listening to patients' prose all the time an entrée into new ways of looking at what they are hearing and also at what they themselves are saying. These new methods bring perforce the kind of self-consciousness to the clinical process which may make one stumble at times, but offers in the end a vital, new, rational form for understanding the underpinnings of the necessary vehicle of our trade—language.

There are also historical reasons why language study may be important to psychotherapeutic clinicians. Our daily activity involves the understanding of symbolic processes, and language organization and structure are our chief data for such expression. Moreover, the development of language permits us to have an observable changing datum, to which we may direct our genetic point of view, which has been so vitally embodied in such concepts as regression, fixation, fantasy, and reality acquisition and also in the very structure of our concepts of personality and psychology. For example, the elaboration of ego psychology by Hartmann offered clinicians the possibility of adapting to and integrating much data taken from general psychology. In that sense, he took psychoanalysts and clinicians, in general, away from the central role of conflict in symptom and character formation. He also offered the opportunity to view psychic structure and organization from the standpoint of ego functions and adaptation. It is largely from the later vantage point that psychoanalytic ideas have blossomed into a modern science of the mind and behavior, enabling extension to a variety of psychotherapeutic endeavors. By making linguistic data central to our broadened observational field, we have an area of competence that is particularly human to study and through which meaning is conveyed. The knowledge gained by linguists and psychologists about the way in which language is organized, develops, and fragments cannot but help to enrich our clinical purview. It is to this aim that this volume is directed.

1

The Developmental Point of View
Why Choose Language?

The genesis of language is not to be sought in the prosaic, but in the poetic side of life.

—Otto Jespersen, 1964, p. 433.

Twentieth-century clinical psychiatry in America, and to some degree on the European continent, is permeated by the developmental point of view. The varying influences on clinical practice which stem from psychoanalysis and, in its best sense, behaviorism require full knowledge of the individual's past as well as his present circumstances to illuminate his current behavior. These influences include stored experiences, memories, and their affect on perceptual, cognitive, and emotional organization. Even when the behaviorist approaches the patient from the standpoint of his symptoms, it is necessary, in the course of his work, to enumerate the varying influences and past response patterns of the patient to his symptoms so that the therapist can construct a hierarchy of responses which will help the patient understand the ramifications and variations of the desensitization process that ensues.

Psychoanalysis has clearly rested its central theoretical tenets on a genetic point of view. Freud discovered that repressed and unconscious wishes and ideas were stimulated during circumstances of traumatic disequilibrium occurring during childhood. Although in his *Studies on Hysteria* (1893–1895/1955) Freud did not trace the traumatic occurrences below the age of eight, he later postulated, in the case of the wolf man (1918/1955), that there were earlier infantile experiences which were significant and relevant to adult symptom formation. These effects may be

1

said to act at a distance. But if most causal relationships are obvious to us only because they occur as temporal contingencies, causes acting at a distance are less readily seen—to wit, there are records of tribal peoples who were not aware of the relationship between coitus and birth. Childhood had been ignored for so long that Freud's discovery leading to an increased focus on childhood may be of similar significance to our smug Western minds. Although some subsequent thinkers within psychoanalysis deviated from Freud's general position with regard to libido theory or the economics of mental disturbance, almost none ever gave up the genetic point of view.

Sullivan's (1954) insistence on a careful history and anamnesis not only has its roots in Meyer's (1957) psychobiology, which insisted on a life chart for each patient so that one could understand the genesis, origins, and patterns of an individual's behavior, but also came from the genetic point of view of psychoanalysis. This genetic point of view, however, is not exclusive to psychoanalysis or, for that matter, to modern psychiatry. It has ample and sufficient historical roots in Western and other thinking which should make us stop and take notice that even the vantage point itself has a historical and genetic disposition and did not emerge *ex nihilo*. We may even suggest a historical latency when childhood was thought to be irrelevant.

If we agree with Whitehead's proposition that all philosophy and therefore all science are a series of footnotes to Plato, we must look to the master himself as a precursor to our current point of view. In *The Republic*, Plato (1968) prescribed a method of child rearing that will produce or have the tendency to produce a philosopher king, thereby revealing the surmise that child rearing is a vital determiner of future development of competence as a social being. This proposition was further carried out by Aristotle in a very practical way when he took the responsibility to teach Alexander the Great during the early years of the conqueror's life. We can look to other philosophers for additional verification that what seems to be a very twentieth-century view indeed had its origins in the past. Probably the best summary of this notion was offered by, or attributed to, the Jesuits, who suggested that if one gave a child from one to five years of age to their care they would make a Catholic and a theist of him. However, the people of the Middle Ages were generally supposed to have ignored childhood as a largely irrelevant period of life which demanded no special interest (Aries, 1962). This kind of neglect was certainly not true among the economic and intellectual elite who centered their intellectual hopes in the representatives of the church. For the Church Fathers, education was a primary concern, if guided toward faith as well as reason. Indeed, there is a growing literature that suggests more interest than formerly surmised during the so-called Dark Ages.

The most forthright espousal of the notion that childhood and development are central to good humanity emerged in the period of the Enlightenment when Rousseau (1761/1978), in his book *Emile*, documented the effects of early education on later development. I do not plan to review the entire history of education to justify the developmental point of view, only to offer a longer view of our emergent "modernism." Perhaps Wordsworth (1923) summarized best the central purpose of our concern when he wrote that "the child is the father of the man," and it is in this faith that we use the developmental point of view as a frame of reference for our clinical work.

Turning from the cultural roots of our modernism to biology itself, we find that ontogenesis came to the notice of scientists in the second half of the nineteenth century following Darwin's (1929) discovery of species continuity. It was through the efforts of later biologists that Darwin's concepts of continuity and adaptive variation were used by the comparative anatomists who studied phylogenetic homologies and similarities to establish continuity. With the birth of embryology, Haeckel's (1879) biogenetic law became the watchword of the biological sciences and, to some degree, has remained well into the middle of the twentieth century. Embryology took hold as a mother science because the continuity between and among species could be observed even within a single organism by looking to the earliest developmental stages which, in the human infant, are rushed through during the first three months of gestation. With birth itself, the developmental course had to be looked at in continuity with prior developmental stages and demanded new techniques of observation.

However, this emphasis on continuity in development glossed over the discontinuities in development. Although it is possible to trace a developmental line or see an analogy in structure or even use quantitative methods to show continuous linear relationships, there seemed to be differences in behavior and function which could only be accounted for by a concept of hierarchic integration taking place from period to period. Stage-by-stage developmental advances could be looked at as new achievements that are stacked in an epigenetic sequence, depending on not only the prior experience but also representing a new level of organization with a new capacity for functioning and behaving. Moreover, in this discontinuity, new functional means of adapting to the

world around the organism were achieved—new means, which, although dependent upon the substrate—that is, the brain, or the nervous
system in the case of behavior—were not reducible to it (Werner, 1926).
Helmholz's hope that everything would ultimately reduce to chemistry
had to be replaced with the notion that levels of biological organization
could each be studied in its own right, and whereas the data of one level
ought not contradict the data of the other, the best that could be done
would be to look for a parallelism rather than an isomorphism on a
point-to-point basis between structure and function. Man began to
study psychology as well as biology. Psychology had to be looked at as
more than a branch of epistemology or biology, and new postulates,
new theories, and new interrelationships had to be measured empirically and understood using these new models.

Copernicus set the earth free from man's geocentric view by making
a simpler system, using the sun as the center of the universe, and
thereby displaced man from his former arrogance as the highest creature
on a planet that was the center of the universe. In contrast, psychology
put man again at the center of things as the organizer of his world and as
a relevant focus for study. This was so not only because of what we
shared in relation to our biological continuity with other organisms or
our phylogenetic heritage, but also because in some ways we stood segregated among the species as purveyors of civilization, as *thinkers*, and
as *conscious actors* on and within our ecology, as well as simply reactors
to that ecology. Psychology, in its fullest sense, also sought to study the
limiting factors that distinguish the reactive from the consummatory
behaviors which derive from knowing, planning, and willing. Psychologists learned to distinguish between the apparent similar overlapping
curves of reactivity among and between different species and the substrate or intermediary processes involved in producing that data. The
black box, after all, may be alive with intermediary steps or even intervening variables in behaviorist terms. The mind may be a *plenum of ideas*
as the pre-Socratic philosophers suggested, and yet the behavioral response may be the same. This is the basis within the evolution of
psychological functioning and within the ontogenesis of the individual
with which we establish man at the center of this particular ecological
universe. More specifically, although subject to the same vicissitudes
and threats of environmental annihilation given within this balance with
nature, man is also different from other species because of a number of
significant factors.

One of the factors is represented in man's position as a

symbolizer—and among his symbolic functions, he is a creator of languages. Although these languages may take a number of different forms
and produce a babel of noncommunication between peoples, all lang-
guages are based on a set of uniform principles which can be studied,
elaborated, compared, and, in general, used for investigation of a specific developmental line. We study language for its unique contribution
to our understanding of development and also as an example of the
general principles and factors that exist and influence our understanding
of all developmental lines. It is to this purpose that I will direct this
volume and state its general proposition as follows: If we must select
from a general developmental psychology a structural process that will
best describe the human condition, language is one of those natural
sectors which ought to illuminate man's unique phylogenetic position as
a symbolizer. Psychotherapy as we know it would not be possible were
man not uniquely fitted to this emergent function of symbolizing.

It has been generally stated that, to use symbolic forms, one must
have a medium which provides the possibility for (1) semanticity, (2)
displacement, and (3) productivity. In choosing language development
for our study, we are in some ways obeying Darwin's law of continuity
in that communicative systems of great variety are also available to other
species as well as man. Although they can be described in terms of
stimulus–response behavior, Miller (1964) suggested that these formulations account for only about 10% of human behavior. In that sense,
then, we will take man away from his continuity and present symbolization as a discontinuous emergent function. For example, consider a
number of circumstances which human beings encounter in their day-
to-day living in relation to psychiatrists and therapists, in which the
circumstances of semanticity, displacement, and productivity become relevant factors for the way in which their responses are determined.

The specific instance of *who* comes to the psychiatrist, and *under
what circumstances*, provides a practical matter for consideration in our
overview. Clearly, the answer to these queries are determined by a
number of factors that are dependent not only on the stimulus to search
for a physician or therapist, such as pain, or illness, or discomfort, or
symptom formation, but also on the meaning (that is, the *semanticity*) of
the designation "being ill," or "being in mental pain," or "suffering."
An important historical example is available in the attitudes of the
populace to the condition of childbed (puerperal) fever during the
nineteenth century. Although hospitals were generally set up as places
for comfort and as havens, it was well known among pregnant women

that having their babies at home would lead to more salutary circumstances *post partum* than in seeking hospital confinement. The hospital
was looked upon as a death trap, with serious doubt as to whether a
return home would ever occur, and, as such, many women did not go to
hospitals or to physicians. The unknown factors of the etiology of puerperal fever, as a transmitted bacterial infection due to poor sanitary
conditions, remained, at that time, obscure. However, the empirical fact
that death following childbirth occurred in hospitals became an aversive
memory which urged many women to stay at home. Hospitals thus
became identified with death after childbirth, and this identification and
its social dissemination were dependent upon the concept of the "meaning of the hospital" to an individual and his ability to transmit that
impression to others in his community. The avoidance action would not
have been taken if the understanding, linkage, and causal relationship
had not been established. It became symbolic, if you will, of death. It
stood for something other than what was the structure or intent of
hospitals. Moreover, there is no valid reason, for example, why the
vocal or graphic configuration "hospital," a pile of generally red bricks
housing beds arranged in wards, with patients ministered to by nurses
and practicioners of "physic and chirurgy," should stand for dying except that man had made an associative and affective link and had responded to it accordingly. He designated it finally as a meaningful configuration which stood for death.

If one were to make an iconic representation of this situation in a
cartoon, one would see, for example, a representation of the hospital and
a dead, pregnant woman. The reader would easily understand its meaning. It would be a pictorial symbol with an immediate relationship to
that which the picture stood for based on past tragedy. One might even
surmise that, at times, social avoidance of this sort could occur on a
misapprehension of a single, disturbed, delusional individual. Some
climates, such as seventeenth-century Salem, Massachusetts, supported
such distortions to mass hysteria. Moreover, once the link—hospital
equals death—was made, it is conceivable that some might act as though
the past fact were still functional even long after that relationship no
longer held in fact. Man's very tendency toward history collecting would
then become more important than his capacity for immediate, empirical
fact-finding as a generator of behavior.

Another example of this possibility for symbolization and how
meaning influences behavior can be found in the instance of why
mothers of children who have exanthemata call a physician. An interest-

ing study entitled "The Health of Regionville" (Koos, 1954) described some of the factors that determine whether or not mothers go to physicians, chiropractors, or druggists in their community and which hospitals they use. Among the factors that Koos studied was physican utilization. It was striking that most mothers whose children had measles, or chicken pox, or any of the other exanthematous diseases knew these complaints were self-limiting with a finite course. They nevertheless contacted physicians to have their children examined. When they were asked why this was the case, they suggested that they were interested in their image in the community and did not want to appear to their neighbors as neglectful parents. In this instance, they viewed their search for a doctor as a symbolic statement to their neighbors that they were careful and concerned parents. The behavior itself had very little to do with the well-being or care of the child but became a kind of social document of their interest in child rearing, since most mothers were unaware of the dire consequences following some cases of measles or chicken pox that some 20 years later gave rise to mandatory immunization for the former.

At yet another level, one can look at the differential tolerance between ghetto and middle-class families for hyperactive behavior in children and whether they seek medical or psychological help. It is well known that a middle-class child who acts up a bit and is rambunctious and overactive will be brought to a physician more readily than a ghetto child. The meaning of the active behavior in the parent's understanding of disturbance is rather a remote possibility for the ghetto parent compared to the middle-class or educated parent. Thus, the behaviors of the individuals involved in seeking physicians or psychological aid are highly dependent on what the behavior means, what the activity means, and what the institutions of psychiatry, psychology, or social service are seen to provide. This is not a simple associative scheme; this is not a simple concomitance of conditioned and unconditioned responses. It involves a long history of exposure to empirical facts within the society itself as well as the establishment of meaning within individuals and families concerning each of the elements involved. Thus, the *semanticity* (the meaning function of language) is of paramount importance to man's clinical behavior and, more than anything else, determines whether or not he goes to the physician, no less than to a psychiatrist. Up to this point, I have only noted the conscious sphere of semanticity ignoring, for the present, unconscious factors.

The second factor of *displacement* of linguistic forms refers to the ability to rerepresent an idea, or idea of a behavior, apart from the initial circumstance where it was first elicited. The concept may also refer to the capacity to represent the same meaning in a number of different vehicles. For example, our linguistic system permits representation of an idea or mental event in a sound trace in the vocal-auditory sphere and then in a picture or a graphic representation as a row of alphabetic letters. Displacement offers a possibility for economy of action—so much can be condensed, sorted, and transferred in compact units that it is amazing how we marvel at the efficiency of computers when language has been our legacy since evolution left us in our current form. Moreover, we may use a symbol at time A to represent a contemporaneous event and then bring it out at time B and refer back to A or reapply it anew. Displacement requires memory storage and makes history possible. The equation previously noted concerning the word hospital= death may still be applied by some who are unaware of the vast changes in hospital sanitation since Semmelweiss and Lister. He may displace his formerly appropriate response to new sanitary hospitals, thereby acting as if words remained fixed in meaning and did not respond to a changing world. Similarly, if *psychiatrist* means "a physician who deals with the insane," the individual with problems in the 1970s may demure seeking aid because he or she is not "crazy." This variety of displacement of meaning results from ignorance of change in meaning over time.

Another less pathological displacement more significant to linguistics refers to the ability of the individual to talk about events while they are not immediately in his experience. The entire structure of talking about something and not doing something is a legacy of having language at our disposal with which to do it. These very capacities to store and displace are necessary to a higher-order mental function that may result in the possibility of generativity or productivity in language use.

This third factor of *productivity* involves the ability to put together the elements of a particular vehicle of representation into new and creative forms which are used for coding ideas as relationships (logical, causal, etc.) on the spot, in unique or unusual configurations. We could not generate novel sentences without this ready capacity nor could we invent new, logical, mathematical or *a priori* systems which delight our mathematicians and linguists. If the words we use could not be joined to say new things, we would be victims of continuously having to use old rigid formulas to describe new situations. Language would be a static template dependent on a large number of fixed phrases. The process would be as inflexible and unparsimonious as a set of ideographs rather than a phonetic alphabet.

It is tempting to question whether we may compare the human-language function, using these three factors of semanticity, displacement, and productivity, to the capacities of other species to strengthen our notion of human language as a discontinuous function that provides man with a hierarchic advantage. This, indeed, has already been done by some observers. In their quest for certainty about the unique humanness of the symbolizing aspects of language, researchers have tried to teach other species behaviors or skills that would be comparable to language. The familiar circus horse who does arithmetic and other examples of this kind are likely progenitors of this enterprise. Subsequent chapters will deal with this matter more fully, especially the recent studies of teaching "language" to primates.

Thus far, we have stressed the usefulness of language as a hierarchically superior system available as a code for communication between individuals. However, we respond not only to external symbols and stimuli but also to internal cues, recognized or unrecognized. Talking within, or inner dialogue, has the potential to be an important determinant of our human behavior, all the more so as development proceeds. These inner dialogues are also organized according to systems of meaning which follow the rules of language, more or less. Moreover, there are subsystems, such as fantasy and other inner mentation, that we can study apart from their main system. These have become important to the psychiatrist who is curious about depth psychology. Lacan (1956) and others who are less radically linguistic go so far as to suggest that the unconscious is structured like a language.

Another primary distinction concerns the difference between speech and language. Briefly, speech may be seen as the acoustic-vocal event which has rules for shape but would be empty of meaning if a language were not behind it. The rules pertain to structure and organizational features that can be analyzed for their uniqueness or universality. If language is constituted by such a scheme as outlined, then its features and rules for harmony and right soundingness could be derived from any single language and become our tools of study. These properties of language as a system will help us organize our current investigation.

To simplify a complex field into more manageable units which will be familiar to clinicians, let us return to the developmental propositions that are common to both developmental linguistics and clinical psychiatry. We can proceed from the general developmental notion that language, like other developing functions, takes form in (1) a socialized cultural code which is subject to the (2) viscissitudes of central nervous system maturation and ego structuralization, and that, in turn, (3) these two factors converge in development in the patterning which begins to take place in an infant and child, first on its mother's lap and later at her knee.

1. Our particular language behavior emerges directly from a common socialized code which is provided to us by our culture. One may well ask how did each culture arrive at its particular language form? After all, there are differences—some languages prefer adjectives before and some after their nouns—some languages are highly and others less highly infected, etc. One could easily resort to the myth of the Tower of Babel as a means of understanding what many linguists have studied for so long. There are probably as many studies concerning the origin of language, which include such ideas as a common protolanguage later differentiating into many forms or multiple sources for major language groups, as there are grains of sand. As clinicians, we are not much interested in this sector of knowledge, but sometimes historic study provides models applicable to individual study. Freud's (1907/1959) brilliant analysis of cultural, ritual, and individual compulsion provides an interesting example of such modeling.

Among the popular beliefs concerning the earliest forms of language was a notion that all words started out as onomatopoeic representations; that is, the words imitated in their sound patterns the things or events represented. A word such as "whinny" is a mimicry of the sound that the horse makes. The word becomes a vocal icon of the thing represented. However, the problem remains that most phonetic forms seem to be arbitrary rather than related in this simple form of sound symbolism. With this example from historic linguistics, a problem of individual development is sharpened: What is the relationship of the socialized cultural code to the actual things of the world apprehended by the senses? The code we use has pointing or designating functions and stands for actions, things, ideas, and relationships that exist in an external world or in the inner world as an aspect of man's organizing capacities. If this indeed were not the case, it would also not be the case that language facility and utilization would be so valuable and economic a tool for man in his attempt to manipulate his world. Problems of reference require special treatment and understanding for psychotherapists and are treated more extensively in Chapters 6 and 8.

2. The second proposition indicates that the capacity for language is

subject to the vicissitudes of central nervous system (CNS) maturation and the autonomous ego functions for cognition which are dependent on CNS development. This is postulated on the basis that language develops in a biological substrate as an emerging system which is dependent not only on cultural input but also on postulated, innate, preformist capacities for linguistic competence. In recent years, the work of Lenneberg (1967) and the suggestions of Chomsky (1965) support the propositions that the rules for organizing words into sentences (grammar and syntax) are also dependent on biological maturational structures. The simple fact that a naming explosion takes place in children between 18 months and three years of age, coordinated with a syntactic explosion during the same period regardless of languages spoken and cultural setting, is suggestive of a universal human timetable. The emergence of a capacity for understanding and stating relational aspects between things is coordinated with those events. The skill in relating subject, action, and object in words occurs in a rather fixed sequential form and evolves into later abilities for stating coordinated relations, subordinate changes, and contigency statements. The apparent fixity of sequence, as in Piagetian psychology, is best accounted for by a biological timetable which provides a syntactic sequencing ego structure. The subtleties of controversy between preformism and learning will not be discussed here. Suffice it to say that language development and use seem to demand, at the least, a primate brain for natural languages to develop without supraspecies instruction. The human brain must also undergo maturation within a human social context as essential to language development and capacity for linguistic performance.

Much as we may look at the factors already mentioned as being dependent on biological maturation, it is certainly evident that children who are brought up in the English-speaking world speak English just as children who are brought up by mothers who speak Oriental languages also speak Oriental languages. The patterning of specific language behavior takes place in accord with the cultural pattern with the mother as the cultural agent to the child. As such, the biological unit of mother and child, which was parasitically arranged during the intrauterine life, can be extended significantly as an important factor of the early extrauterine symbiotic tie *postpartum*. The phonetic specificity of a particular language is certainly socially conveyed by the mother, whereas the capacity for phonetic differentiation into recognizable vocal-articulatory signs is perhaps biological. The reinforcement of particular phonetic forms emerging into phonemic patterns is culturally determined. Phonemic specificity resulting from the first interactions evolve into later communicative skills. The variations in "good enough mothering" permits small or great exposure to the tones of the mother tongue or rich or poor variation in the multiple forms possible. How people use language in a practical manner as a means of exchange clearly has its origins in these early interactions. But, as a developmental principle, it should be clear that what emerges are phonemic competencies that are more than the sum of their origins and not reducible to these origins in an additive way. This is so because the small differences we recognize as native speakers of a language allow more than phonetic discrimination. They emerge into semantic distinctions of great consequence.

Communication *per se* is, however, not unique to the human species; communication via vocal forms is also shared with other species at differing phyletic levels, but the specific vocal forms of phonemically discrete language does seem to be unique to human beings. In fact, it is this duality of patterning which Hockett (1960) claimed distinguishes the human species from all others. An example of duality of patterning is the difference between *pin* and *bin* or *nib* and *bin*. The sound forms of human language are so exquisitely detailed and the perceptual organization of the receiver must be so constructed that, given these small perceptual variations, the cognitive impact is to register a difference in meaning when the message is decoded. This represents a great flexibility and potential for generativity even at a phonetic level.

Finally, then, language can be looked at as a complex system created by human beings that emerges from the preserved operation of many functions enabling us maximum flexibility in manipulating our world. Language is therefore ideal as a dimension for study in elaborating what is most characteristically human and has the virtue of a developmental sequence and pattern that may illuminate the process of development itself. Language is (1) a complex organization which involves motor control, cognitive structuring, and social determinants and influences. (2) Language evolves over time and can be studied as its structure changes, as it increases its lexicon, yielding stage- and phase-specific performances as data. In fact, it can be put into Schneirla's (1961) definition of development in that it is a "changing structure of a function over time." As such, it can be related to chronological age and also necessarily related to hierarchic integration of cognitive and ego structures. (3) Language is evolutionarily specific relating to a specific form at a specific level of phylogenetic development and evolving to a particular structural and functional organization which is somewhat discontinuous from other lower-level communicating organizations. And (4), language is dependent on a complex organizational structure which includes the relation of words to a message and even has design features that provide the possibility for productivity and generativity. These phenomena make language an apt area occurring naturally and having a structural organization against which we may measure deviation. We can observe not only how language evolves in particular individuals over time, but we can also see how particular individuals under different variations of rearing practices devolve to specific kinds of usage. Linguistic analysis may then prove an unmined area that psychotherapists ought to explore to learn more about their patients who tend to use speech and language in their efforts at psychic repair.

In this first chapter, I have offered a possible structure for the study of language and have organized the existing ideas and data on language development in such a way that the remainder of this presentation will allow the reader to see the use of linguistic development as an important tool for learning about developmental principles, not only for clinical understanding but also as a means of studying the developmental process itself.

2

What Is Language and How Do We Look at It?

We have DNA for grammar, neurons for syntax. We can never let up; we scramble our way through one civilization after another, metamorphosing, sprouting tools and cities everywhere, and all the time new words keep tumbling out.

—Lewis Thomas, 1974, p. 129.

Everyone seems to have a general understanding that he or she speaks a language, or, if a polyglot, many languages. Common sense usually suggests that a language serves the purpose of communication. However, it is also common to encounter extensions of the term *language* in such phrases as the language of love, the language of the birds, the language of mathematics. These extensions may be metaphoric and make for a quandary as to how to limit the term so that its extensions and applications do not add to our confusion. This chapter will address the issue of clarifying terms and applying a number of frames of reference to see if they aid in systematizing the data available on language.

On a phenomenological level, we can isolate certain events and call them speech events, which then can be looked at as examples of language. For example, let us consider the following therapeutic encounter in a specific language context. We may be able to piece together the elements relevant to the therapeutic exchange and determine how and where they cut across linguistic lines. The therapist has just made an intervention which he designates as an interpretation which, in this instance, involves bringing together a number of apparently disparate remarks, made by the patient, into a coherent unified phrase with logical connections. Following the interpretation the patient says, "Now, that is really an interpretation!" If we were writing stage directions for the circumstance, we might want to describe the tone of his remarks and the degree of affirmation exposed in the melody of the response. The stage directions might also read that the comment is delivered with irony.

In a second example of a therapeutic exchange, during the course of associations in a psychoanalysis (which sometimes has the feeling of an extreme form of isolated monologue), a patient says that he "practices *manipulatio cum manibus*" while he fantasies that he is engaged in the "coital act with the maternal object." These examples of a language exchange are understandable; we can comprehend their meaning directly, but the particular form of delivery does not permit us to say very much about what constitutes the choices involved in the latter individual's word selection or in the former patient's performance of the stage directions. One of the achievements of linguistics, especially since the time of Saussure, involves the distinction between speech and language. Although our common-sense, day-to-day use of language does not demand such a distinction, theory building is advanced if we can focus on smaller units of observation.

Ferdinand de Saussure, a Swiss grammarian who lived between 1857 and 1913, wrote his *Course in General Linguistics* (1959), which incorporates lectures delivered between 1906 and 1911. He was a contemporary of Freud's, and the fact that Freud's *Introductory Lectures on Psychoanalysis* (1915–1916/1963) was written in 1916 places both of them as intellectual innovators attempting to disseminate their ideas in Middle Europe within the same zeitgeist. Saussure invoked the distinction between *la langue* (language) and its particular form *la parole* (speaking) to inform us that speech is a particular mixture of physical, physiological, psychological, and social factors which may not concern us in our investigation of language as an institution and as a formal system. Speaking is studied by different methods than is language. Language may be viewed as a systematic, codified area for study that was, by and large, ignored until Saussure effected his distinction.

When considered as distinct from speech, language consists of a code governed by rules of order and possesses regularities that may enable us to discover universal formalisms that dictate its structure regardless of which particular language we speak. Speech, on the other hand, reduces to the moment-to-moment performance of that language. Rosen (1966) described speech as the "acoustical forms of words" and sometimes the vocal-articulatory process needed for the production of words. Saussure invoked a striking simile referring to language as a symphony, and speech as the particular performance of that symphony. By extending the simile to the work done by different disciplines, linguists tend to study the score and its harmonies, whereas psychologists study performance to infer psychological and social processes, and speech and hearing therapists study intelligibility and communicative efficacy or dysfluency.

Even though modern linguists choose to study structure, this has not always been the case. Languages also undergo changes in use over long time spans, and linguists, at other times, have taken the lawfulness of such changes as the object of their interest. The changes, both in structure and in lexical content, may obey universal laws of drift but tend to be inaugurated in specific languages that give rise to language families. The data are available, since written language permits us to study literature as examples of language. Shakespearean English, Chaucerian English, Anglo Saxon, and perhaps proto-German are examples of altering structures under the impact of time. This type of study is called *diachronic linguistics*. We can also examine the variations in structure within a static period which involve current variants within a language structure that are permitted by rules governing use. The study of language during one time period is called *synchronic linguistics*. Speech, on the other hand, may be rich, varied, idiosyncratic—an argot, a jargon, or a local dialect. All varieties of speech, however, use as a base the formalisms of the particular language we can study structurally. In the third and fourth quarters of this century, the disciples of Saussure who remained in structural linguistics have made advances attempting to look at how particular speech patterns, or particular speech events, or particular speech periods relate to the general formalisms of language itself. Attempts have also been made to make the studies more scientific by applying statistical and other methods.

The paths taken are varied. Some investigators sought to build a systematic study of language by postulating molecular and atomistic structures that underlie molar units, such as sentences. Other researchers approached the matter from larger units and then sought to find a more fundamental base structure that organizes particular linguistic forms in their infinite variety. Chomsky (1957) provided us with another dichotomy which overlaps with Saussure's language and speech in a number of ways. He talks of a competence–performance split. He and his followers insist that a particular performance of a language is only a single example of a general linguistic capacity which he calls *competence*. He dissociates his competence from Saussure's *la langue* by suggesting that the former includes a system of generative processes rather than a static inventory of items in a system (Chomsky, 1965). Competence, while it may develop, is viewed as an innate given in the average expectable biological equipment of normal human beings. Lenneberg's (1967) biodevelopmental studies tend to be an apology for this argument in its strong form. Thus, researchers of pure linguistics do not choose to study the data of development of language, for example, or the data of productions of individuals on the couch, because the data they recently find interesting are much closer to logical formulas and intuitions concerning grammaticality. Instead, they seek to find that minimal set of rules which organizes the linguistic world of individuals no matter what language they speak.

This distinction between production and competence is important, because many of the matters that will be touched on, regarding the use of linguistic theory as applied to clinical practice, will not correspond to the competence–performance distinction. Moreover, in applying an abstract model based on different data, we have to anticipate adjustments prior to trying the model for fit to another data base. Linguists, in their purest working conditions, prefer to have a sentence on a 3×5 card or a blackboard without its context—without its conditions of performance. Such a procedural restaint would not enable those linguists to approach the two clinical examples cited earlier. These examples, with their accompanying stage directions, represent more data than pure linguistics is currently able to consider. For example, linguists would not want to know about irony. They would not want to know about the character structure that goes with the kind of formalism of the second patient who spoke Latin rather than English. They would take the words, the sentence structure, and the relationships revealed in the grammar as the subject matter to which they would attend. They would look for similarities and differences and congruences in the underlying grammatical structure, searching for deep relationships that bind a variety of natural sentences together. These superficial structures would then be examined in particular productions to see if they fit into the model that demonstrates general competence in the language.

Just as the world is made up of a conglomerate of overlapping events, the scientific world is made up of a number of different disciplines, all of which apparently attend to the same event. Because a large part of the data base of human psychology, and medical psychology especially, has, for so long, been speech and language production, the

In 1966, Rosen tried to use his observations of language distortion in psychoanalytic patients to illuminate a variety of "ego deviations." He noted that, in addition to Freud's failure to consider the distinction between speech and language, Freud had also missed what Ogden and Richards had elaborated in terms of how the thing–presentation is psychologically represented. Moreover, he said that disturbances of communication would also need clarification by consideration of the ontogenesis of the relation of word to thing and the problems that we encounter when we look at preverbal thought in relation to preintellectual speech and the later elaboration of each.

The Ogden–Richards scheme leaves open the essential question of how words came to stand for ideas or things in the first instance (that is, the ontogenetic query raised by Rosen) and how particular individuals, qua individuals, begin to think about the world in categories as opposed to concrete images. In his *Republic*, Plato suggested that the ideas were *most real* rather than the particular form of the ideas. As an example, if I think of a particular Louis Quatorze chair as it is presented to me in a dream or as a free image in therapy, I may have a string of associations which direct me to where I saw that chair, who I saw sitting in it last, or a period of history when the excesses of the court of King Louis correspond to wishes for similar overindulgence on my part. On the other hand, when I think of *chair*, I do not necessarily have in mind one particular chair, Louis Quatorze or other. But even the very word *chair* seems to have no essential relation to either a Louis Quatorze, or Eames, or Breuer, or Mies van der Rohe chair. However, many researchers in linguistics have suggested that, though there is no apparent relationship between word and thing, there must be a hidden relationship between the sound formation of "chair" and the particular object or idea that it stands for. We do know a class of words immediately related to the sounds to which they refer: the onomatopoeic words—babble, slur, and crack—are but a few examples of this variety of sound symbolism. The implication of such a theory would be that words and things are historically related.

During the late nineteenth century, the *Académie Française* refused all papers which had to do with the origin of language and sound symbolism. At that time, the theories and the hopes were that, if one examined the history of a particular word, its etymological origins, and its historical roots, one would find some natural relationship between sounds and the things they signified. More recently, a series of experiments were carried out in which scientists concocted sets of "nonsense syllables," that is, the sound patterns had no conventional meaning in that language, and asked subjects to consider their meaning. Often the nonsense syllables were paired pseudowords and differed in only one feature, a vowel or a consonant. For example, "Is bim larger or smaller than bam?" Most people answered in statistically significant numbers that /bim/ was smaller than /bam/ or that if /bim/ or /bam/ had to be an elephant or a mouse, that it was more likely that /bam/ was the elephant and /bim/ the mouse. Although these experiments provided some basis for belief in sound symbolism, the data did not hold up across the language families or when the universe of choices for matching was broader than pairs.

Where then does the sense of naturalness in our language come from, if sound symbolism does not hold? (Part of this answer will come from the developmental studies to be considered later in this volume.) For the present, and briefly stated, Werner and Kaplan (1963) suggested that there is a physiognomic apprehension of words in addition to cognitive categorization from earliest learning, and that words do not stand for things simply as labels tacked on to percepts or experiences. The relevance to therapists of such a formulation is that words are dynamically schematized in affective constellations as well as intellectually schematized by virtue of the sound's association to a meaning in a specific or idiosyncratic sense (see Chapter 6). Having introduced some rich potential study, I will stimulate further interest and turn to another study that has its own promise. This study followed a model that prevailed in chemistry, physics, and later in molecular biology. It was a method that promised the scientific rigor of those sciences. The model suggested essentially that the smallest building blocks of any particular complex structure might best be broken down to ever smaller units arranged in a hierarchy.

Bloomfield (1933) proposed that like atoms the smallest units of speech might be built into the equivalent of molecules, elements, compounds, etc., and that emergent complexity might yield an understanding of the operations and functions of these smaller units and their rules of synthesis. In considering such a model, one must remember that the interval between Saussure and Chomsky was a period of great ferment with an emphasis on unity of science and a hope that the method of physics might underlie all knowledge. Anthropologists were in the field, listening to foreign undeciphered languages, taking them down in phonetic notation without knowledge of segmentation of the language into word boundaries. Starting with the smallest sound units that were distinguishable to a native speaker, linguists discovered or created *phonemes*; each phoneme was then recorded and looked at and compared from language to language. The linguists found striking evidence that each language was made up of only a finite number of phonemes compared to the great number of words that were available within that language. Indeed, each language had barely 30 of these units. Moreover, psychologists found that native speakers using a particular language could not easily learn the phonemic pattern of another language without accent after reaching their eleventh birthday. This seemed a plausible and fruitful route if it rendered such simplicity. The next unit considered was the *morpheme*, the smallest unit which carried meaning, and so on up the line to a word, and then from a word to a sentence or *tagmeme*. Thus, the very scaffolding of a theory of linguistics based on ever smaller units was created. This led to a kind of molecularization of language and the unification of varying molecules into substances which common sense could apprehend.

If we look at the two clinical examples cited earlier and try to find from those whether we have any better understanding based on this model of what the individual said, we will find it yields little for us as clinicians. Chomsky (1957), on the other hand, returned essentially to Saussure's hope stating that language could be examined as a competence–performance scheme. This scheme offered the notion that surface forms—those very units and elements which were attended to so strongly by Bloomfield—were significant. However, they were the more significant if compared to what he called the *deep structural organizations of language*. Thus, the particular form of a sentence or the particular words an individual used helped very little in the linguistic unraveling of its significance or its anomaly or ambiguity. We, instead, might reduce all surface structures to some base hypothetical deep structure which then could be looked at as corresponding to units that the mind itself uses to analyze and comprehend. As such, we could hear the sentences taken from the clinical examples which bore irony or the second patient's comment in Latin as understandable from a linguistic standpoint, but only fully understandable when we examine aspects of the productions that are orthogonal to linguistics, that is, travel a parallel route but not essential to linguistic studies. As a discipline, linguistics had to admit that its study focus was narrower than production and that common day-to-day grasp of meaning might be mediated by more than one system.

The significance of the choice of the Latin phrase by our patient as opposed to a non-Latin phrase lies not in the realm of linguistics but elsewhere. These extra linguistic matters are significant to therapists because they are the sustenance of our work. But we could not survive on only the study of choices or the music and ironic features; we would still have to understand the words, too, and the sentences in which they are embedded. It is easy to recognize that we have run through a number of ways that scientists have looked at language none of which seems to suit us directly as therapists. As a beginning in the ordering of this apparent chaos, I would quote Charles Morris (1964), who talked about three varieties of problems which could be studied using three different approaches: (1) the problem of the relationship of words to things—we have already alluded to in the first section of this chapter when we talked about problems of reference; (2) the relationship between words and words, to which Chomsky and the modern linguists are so devoted is found in the study of syntax and grammar; and (3) the relationship of words to people—this Morris calls *pragmatics*. That he termed this area pragmatics is probably a result of the spirit of William James who had made of language a central concern for his viewpoint. We can now call these areas communication sciences or *information theory*, which would include all the models that are available by which individuals understand each other and are able to encode and decode linguistic propositions. The aforementioned notwithstanding, Morris's categorical breakdown into these three areas can serve as a formal set of distinctions that can be used as a guide throughout the remainder of this book. This set of distinctions with which we can segment our thoughts should delineate the particular problems that accrue from each study area and their application to theory as applied to therapeutic discourse.

Although I have not explained the use of irony or the Latinisms by the two patients, I have used the productions to suggest possible ways for therapists to look at them as data that have not been explored much in theories of therapeutic interaction that exclude language. In therapy, this provides us with a way of looking at language in action which involves the introduction of new schemata to enable us to attend to the stuff we work with, mainly words. It is a schema which should be useful in making relevant distinctions that will help psychotherapists to understand more accurately what they are hearing from their patients and to categorize more precisely what they are hearing into structures and organizations significant for their day-to-day work. If I can convince therapists of that, then the task undertaken in these pages is a useful one.

Language and Psychology

Feeling is a verbal noun—a noun made out of a verb, but psychologically makes an entity out of a process.

—Susanne K. Langer, 1967, p. 20.

Miller (1964) wrote that "a logician is interested in discovering the rules for valid inference, but whether people actually use those rules or not does not concern him" (p. 93). We have here the crux of the issue. Does our study of linguistic analysis have any relevance to psychology? The issue is an epistemological concern that asks if the analysis of a text by logical or grammatical rules is actually mapped onto some variety of psychological structure or apparatus. Can we take rules derived from understanding grammatical form or syntax and the rules of reference and find both psychological and biological correlates that describe the substrate which subsumes that process? Unfortunately, at this time, there is as much sectarianism among linguists as there is among the various psychological schools. The question of whether or not linguistics is mapped onto psychological structures must be posed in this form: Linguistics according to whom? Mapped onto whose version of psychology?

If we start with the psychological theory that espouses the fewest assumptions, we ought to consider the behaviorist model. Although behaviorism was not the first model for thinking about language development and language organization, it certainly was stripped of superordinate constructions and amenable to experimental elaboration. In a way, Miller's comments in Chapter 2 also presage the important notion that stimulus–response behaviorism accounts for some of our linguistic behavior but probably a small portion when compared to the rich inference and theorizing offered by other schools. Behaviorism has not only offered a strong and productive vision within psychology, but scientists who espouse that point of view have provided us with some interesting data regarding what Skinner was later to call *verbal behavior*. The general aim of the behaviorists is to form a model capable of experimental investigation for psychology. As such, they deal with observable stimulus and response sets and eschew the invisible as mystical. When the data arising from the stimulus conditions presented do not fully account for the emergent response, they make mathematical adjustments that have referents derivable from empirical observations which may then be presented in mathematical equations as intervening variables. Behaviorists are rather stringent about these intervening variables, denying them the status of structures or reifying them as organizations within the hypothetical "black box" that is said to be between stimulus (S) and response (R).

When the simple S → R equations did not correspond to the empirical data, early behaviorists suggested that S might be broken into a number of S variables (S_1, S_2, S_3, ... S_4) in order to account for the outcome that was observed. These variables were especially relevant when dealing with aspects of human language behavior, because the early hope that pigeons and rats would be like humans was valid only in a limited sense. When dealing with the understanding of language responses, S_m (S *meaning*) was introduced as one of the intervening variables to be measured; that is, the responses achieved could only be predicted if *meaning* was included in the equations. A similar adjustment was made in Pavlovian psychology when language was taken into consideration by designating it as a second signal system having a significant role in mediating human behavior.

Osgood's (1957) later creation of the semantic differential was an experimental psychologist's attempt to "measure" meaning. He presented subjects with a number of polar words in varying categories and asked them to decide if the presented word corresponded to one or another of these polar dyads or fell between in a neutral position. For example, given a word such as *mother* and a choice between "black and white," or "sweet and sour," or "hard and soft," the subject was expected to locate the word within the domain of those dimensions on a 7-point scale. The pattern that emerged was looked at as a measure of that individual's psychological grasp of the word including some of its connotative richness. After longitudinal pilot work, the following classes of poles were adopted: *evaluative, activity,* and *potency* (e.g., evaluative:

good–bad; activity: active–passive; potency: strong–weak). This approach offered a repeatable procedure with a set number of variables but also offered an opportunity for measurement of language behavior in adults to account for nuances of meaning within the prescribed limits.

The popular adolescent game of symbolism also provides a similar possibility for classification. The individual who is *it* tries to determine the unknown person's name and traits by asking the game opponent, "If he were a cigarette, which brand would he be" or "If a car, what make," etc. Procedures such as the semantic differential offer valid and important experimental properties to understand meaning and suggest that language, at least in its referential network, is, indeed, somewhere embedded onto psychological structures which have existence other than the formal dimensions of text analysis attended to by linguists.

On the syntactic side, word-association tests indicate that subjects provide associations that may be paradigmatic or syntagmatic: in the former instance the word *table* might elicit *furniture* as a response but a syntagmatic response might elicit *legs* or *eat* (table *has* legs; eat *at* table). These latter responses tend to occur early in life, whereas the paradigmatic or classificatory responses cluster after the seventh year.

A clinical therapist should realize that words carry psychological significance as well as an affective impact. If this were not so, we certainly could not influence others by our words—either socially by verbal propaganda, or rhetoric, or in therapy—and the psychological relevance of words and language would have to be considered zero. In fact, the very proposition that talking therapies work is dependent on some psychological mapping of linguistic variables which can account for the varied degree of impact that is recorded. Whether the impact is short- or long-lived is irrelevant to this proposition. Again, the question is whether or not the variables we study linguistically are relevant for a better understanding of psychological organizations and can ultimately be applied in a practical manner by therapists.

A longer view of communicative systems in biology is a warranted digression at this point. In their hope for continuity between other varieties of communication up and down the phylogenetic scale, some investigators made extravagant claims regarding the linguistic communication system of adult human beings. Communication, is communication, is communication is their general message. Whether you ruffle your feathers, or flap your wings, or waggle as in bee language became a matter of relative indifference. Just as it did not matter whether you spoke black English, French-Canadian English, or the languge of algebra to communicate ideas at varying levels. This led some observers to define the nature of communication systems, in general, rather than homing in on human communication. The shift was away from straightforward linguistics, and the more global query considered was what design features characterize all communicative organizations.

Hockett (1960) described 13 design features of language and examined 8 communicational systems, ranging from crickets through primates, and the overlap and differences found in all these systems. Although humans share a number of design features of communication with other species, only human speech and communication utilized all 13 design features. The 13 features of human language include: (1) vocal auditory channel, (2) broadcast transmission and directional reception, (3) rapid fading, (4) interchangeability, (5) total feedback, (6) specialization, (7) semanticity, (8) arbitrariness, (9) discreteness, (10) displacement, (11) productivity, (12) traditional transmission, and (13) duality of patterning.

The first three features seem to be self-evident in relation to the fact that speech is a sound system. Item 5 refers to the notion that what is said is heard by the same person making the utterance. Interchangeability refers to the possibility of mimicking what was heard. Specificity refers to the economy of the linguistic system which does not require large outlays of energy (see Edelheit, 1969). Discreteness suggests that the simple difference between a voiced and unvoiced labial can create the difference between /p/ and /b/, and this again can signal the difference between the meaning units of such words as *pet* and *bet*. Displacement has been discussed under the idea of reference at a distance, and productivity allows for creative and nonempirical imaginative constructions. Arbitrariness permits a large animal to be designated by a short word and vice-versa. Semanticity is discussed under meaning, and traditional transmission concerns extra-genetic learning.

Although each of the design features may occur in the communicational systems examined in varying combinations, duality of patterning is found solely in human speech and language. *Duality* refers to the simultaneous patterning of language at two levels. Phonemes are a small body of empty, meaningless sound patterns distinguishable as the building blocks of the phonology of speech. Their arrangement, however, yields meaningful units, morphemes, and words; for example, *tack, cat,* and *act* share the same phonemes but vary in meaning. Edelheit (1969) discussed this feature as making possible an unlimited lexicon from a parsimonious pool of message-carrying units.

The tendency to make all communication systems alike by virtue of their stimulus–response arrangements is a different approach from the analysis of mechanisms available for communication outlined by Hockett. One can notice the experimental psychologist at work in the former and the linguist in the latter.

Turning toward the molar level in which therapists might find more comfort, we shall now examine Piaget's (1924/1955) early concern with the nature of human language. In many ways, the giant of genetic epistemology began modestly when examining language use of children. He carefully described the distinction between egocentric and socialized speech and, after deciding on criteria for each, coded the utterances of two children to demonstrate that children under a certain age show a predominant number of productions in the category of egocentric speech which, after 12 years of age, is followed by a predominant corpus of socialized speech. The Soviet psychologist Vygotsky (1962) leveled strong criticism at Piaget's interpretation of the data. He acknowledged that, although Piaget was one of the foremost developmental psychologists, his propositions lacked thoughtfulness and missed the most obvious feature about human language—*its traditional transmission*. His argument was a simple one: How could speech be simply egocentric at the outset when speech itself comes from the social environment, that is, it is a social product the child adopts as his own? In many ways, this criticism *mimicked* the strong form of the behaviorist's psychological argument—a proposition which suggested that what is *in* was once *out*. Thus, so-called inner capacity and its resultant behavioral manifestations should be accounted for on the basis of varying generalization from repeated experience and reenforcement. Vygotsky was not content to leave it at that, however, and suggested that two early developmental capacities should be considered: preverbal thought and preintellectual speech. This split between thought and language was in the psychological air before Vygotsky, but never stated so elegantly.

Early and contemporary psychologists tried to fantasize the nature of the experience of the infant. They came up with comments, such as William James's that it was a blooming, buzzing experience. Vygotsky left open the likelihood that preverbal thought may have some organization of its own. It does not have to be the organization that we are accustomed to in linguistic forms. We could interpolate Freud's discussion of the early organizing effect of the pleasure–unpleasure principle with the predominance of the perceptual system which, in later life, is recathected in dreams as a regression. Specifically, Vygotsky's discussion of Piaget resulted in the notion that, while the child develops a continuous accretion of new verbal forms (or new phonetic mimicries), he gradually begins to match those with, and put them into relation to, already existing thought traces available to him in different, concrete, perceptual forms. Thus, he suggested that speech originally was a path from social development which was then internalized, perhaps even observable, in transitional form as whispers (as Watson suggested) and then utilized for both egocentric and social processes. It left the individual with an accumulation of preverbal episodic memories that psychoanalysts have long regarded as relevant to later development and that are stored in verbal packages. Vygotsky felt that, once the knot between thought and language was tied, we are somehow verbal animals exclusively; we cannot go back. As a developmental psychologist he was not concerned if these earlier forms were available for later use or performance. However, his interest in schizophrenia did suggest that varying coding models could supervene over linguistic coding in disturbed states of mind.

Recent work with patients who have borderline and narcissistic disorders is concerned with the possibility of understanding preverbal organizations, and the injunction to listen to the unconscious demands some alerting as to whether and how we may not only tune in on these presumed prior states but also interpret them. These matters will be examined in Chapters 9 and 10. Langer's (1967) distinction between discursive and nondiscursive thought represents a similar distinction that cannot be ignored. She and others suggested that nonlinguistic (nondiscursive) organization enables us to listen to music and appreciate other art forms with arousal. This dualistic view of human mentation does not cohere with the notion that once the language–intellect knot is tied it creates a complete unity. Recent biological investigation, subsumed under the shibboleth split-brain studies, indicate that there are at least two organizations, even on an anatomical basis, with the left brain as the site of linguistic organizations and the right brain a nonlinguistic organization repository. Controversy and confusion abound in this area of investigation making the distinction less clearcut than initially believed but interesting nevertheless. The Helmholzian dream that Freud himself hoped to unravel and establish in his theory of mind–brain correlates in *A Project for a Scientific Psychology* (1895/1953) is appearing once again. Dualisms continue to abound and threaten our hopes for unity. Both unity and dualism as firm theoretical positions may be motivated by nonlinguistic psychic aims, but our adherence to the data/theory interplay is continually amusing to the observer of the history of science and philosophy. At any rate, both Piaget and Vygotsky, each approaching linguistic performance and its relation to thought in his own way, permitted us to realize that what we are dealing with psychologically is the specific form or organization of representational intelligence and the varying vehicles humans have at their disposal for expression. How can we trace the hierarchic changing organization from preverbal to postverbal periods developmentally, in a manner that would be useful to therapists who must understand human verbalization and behavior in the context of changing life patterns? As elaborated in Chapter 2, the developmental issues are crucial to us, because we would like to be able to point to a variety of regressive modes to which thought and language cling.

Sapir (1921) said that "vocalizations in the beginning are not intended to be directive but are overheard," perhaps as a feature of global motor overflow. A convenient scheme, first elaborated by Buhler (1934), proposed that we designate early vocalizations as *expressive* and that they take on an *appeal* function when the mother begins to recognize and interpret the meaning of the vocal events. Only later does speech become functionally *propositional* and attain a circumstance in which two individuals share their common experience in a socially established code or language.

The early vocalizations of children were studied extensively, and we even know which ones came first, which ones came second, and the timetable of their sequential appearance.[1] In fact, it was the fixed schedule of appearance of linguistic landmarks in infants of all cultures that caused Lenneberg to suggest that these are biological endowments which unfold in essentially average expectable environments. In other words, prior to semantics and syntax, there was something about our oropharyngeal morphology and the development of cerebral dominance and the specialized cortical topography that coordinated centers for speech, temporal pattern arrangements, and sensory and cognitive specialization thus creating the specific sequences of language and speech development. The early vowel and vowel–consonant combinations, available as expressive motor events, progressed to a babbling stage through a jargon phase during the first year of life. The progression to the three-word stage of speech, clearly present by age three,

---

[1]These data are irrelevant to our central purpose but may be pursued in the literature on protolinguistic differentiation.

represented a most remarkable feat. Indeed, the universals of language are such that it was not only the timetable that Lenneberg stressed in his argument for invariability, but also that children have words for relationships between objects and feelings, qualities and actions. They are all constructed according to phonology, syntax, and semantics and, furthermore, all described features can be further elaborated in more abstract terms.

From the clinical standpoint, of course, we are not so much interested in the normative sequence of this development but in what these developmental regularities mean, with respect to the development of the code as a vehicle for mental representation of our experience and significant interaction. Early vowel and consonant sounds are classified by M. M. Lewis (1959) into what he called *comfort* and *discomfort* categories. When the child begins to utter these sounds in a purely expressive manner, their appeal function brings the mother to the infant. Bowlby (1958) remarked that the mother needs the child's cries and smile to bring her halfway, and these early paradigms of social interaction combine with other inborn response systems to result in an attachment.

Social interaction goes on at all levels of experience between mother and infant, but certainly the vocal-auditory level is one with far-reaching consequences considering the central role of language in later social life. Even deaf children babble, but those vocalizations fall off because feedback seems to be necessary for its sustenance and emergence into formed speech. In this early mother–infant matrix of both comtemplating the world together and in making associative sounds, apparently the child, with all its senses intact, begins to recognize and imitate those sounds which have continuing social redeeming factors within a particular code. It is at this point that the phonemic differentiation of a particular language may become established.

By the time phonemes are being registered somewhere during the latter quarter of the first year of life, and by the time the child has between 3 to 50 words in the first year-and-a-half of his life, he is beginning to build a world of contemplative things as opposed to things of action. These latter two constellations we owe to Werner and Kaplan (1963). Similarly, Piaget (1947) suggested that the beginnings of life are sensory-motor, that we begin to encounter the world of syncretic chunks of heterologous moment-to-moment events which are motor as well as sensory and are acted on by a yet indescribable self, and that as development progresses the motor component is gradually stripped from the sensory to leave us with a mental representation. Werner and Kaplan's things-of-action have the characteristics of immediacy, of being sensory-motor, unformed, uncategorized, and context bound. Although things-of-contemplation offered a map of the territory of the reality contemplated, a delay in discharge provided the individual with anticipatory psychological potential. In opposing these two hypothetical moieties, we are opposing polar developmental stages that involve an evolution from the concrete toward the abstract. During this time, the child has integrated a social code (he has tied the knot): he has been enabled to move from immediate experience to distant experience; he can delay things. He can not only delay, but he can displace motor activities into other forms and can *talk about* reality and share propositional language. He no longer has to point at things or to traverse each path separately as though it were unique and without a mental map.

At the same time, Vygotsky's preintellectual speech and other forms of nonlogical organization may prevail in the child's inner life. The child may still retain the magic animism of childhood versus the logical and grammatical form of his word-to-word relationships. He may show that he understands prepositions by responding to requests to put a book *on* a table, but within he may still intermix animate with inanimate, displace danger because of temporal contiguity rather than logical inference, etc. Even in language use the words may be used in as conventional a codelike manner as we would like to think, but full grasp is lacking. For example, Piaget showed that, up to 8 years, the child used *because* in a different manner than used by adults as a dependent causal statement. Moreover, new linguistic acquisitions have specific relationships to the phases of attachment to mother and family. The child possesses a polyphony of expressive possibilities, which includes other modalities than the speech vehicle itself. These developmental matters have a highly specific form in accord with the early interactions between child and mother. Transitional objects and phenomena, for example, have a meaning just as words do, though they are not expressed in the vocal-auditory channel. Turning the passive into the active has an iconic representational value, though it is acted and not said.

As clinicians, we are not so much concerned with formal stages in this development, but only with the correspondence of each stage to its link with psychologically relevant structures and interactional schemata. Of course, if we are child therapists, we would like to know the particular expressive and phonetic and comprehensional capacities of a child at each stage of development. However, as adult therapists, probing the meaning of experience, we are much more interested in how each form of expression is used to convey meaning, and how childhood forms and contents continue to be used in adulthood, and how they can be used to understand their roots in childhood. These are the matters which will determine whether or not we can talk to our patients at the level of the adult or at the level of the child or, more precisely, which developmental level of the child. Each vehicle of expression will determine whether or not a particular image, be it a dream image or otherwise, can be used as a basis that will make sense if we wish to make an interpretation. Moreover, the particular selection of expressive modes from among the many expressive possibilities may be helpful in determining style and character attributes of our patients. For example, will they gesture or will they speak; will they tell us about visual imagery or body sensations; will they cry quietly or tell of their anguish in poetic or abstract language. The one thing that is sure, whichever vehicle patients use and whichever developmental stage it reflects, they all ultimately have to be said in words, because it is in words, using the usual rules of syntax, that we, as clinicians, have to make our constructions.

If we permit our free association or our free-floating attention to dictate the flow of our ideas, the ideas are ultimately expressible in words in the interpretative process in talking therapies. Any approach to the development of the world of contemplation and its particular organization, as well as its idiosyncratic form in a particular individual, has to be translated into the standard language we use for communication. This is so regardless of how sensitive or empathic we claim to be to nonverbal and other cues. Our sensitivities may enable us to listen with "a third ear." In spite of this, I have never heard a therapist talk in other tongues, unless, as in a mystical experience, he claims to be also a mystic or a guru. As such, psychoanalysis and talking therapies are, in essence, rational therapies which follow linguistic rules. We may find something rational in the irrational or the meaning in the apparently meaningless, such as dreams and parapraxes, but we never relinquish the possibility of turning these nondiscursive forms into highly organized, secondary-process, logical propositions. We are interested in the development of logical linguistic forms, not for their own sake but as a means of effectively communicating the illogical aspects of our thinking.

This brings us back to the initial query of whether or not language corresponds to thought. After reviewing the methods used to explore the matter, that is, the developmental sequences in linking and the requirements in therapy, my impression is that they represent separate but overlapping sets. Large areas of thought need not be described by linguistic formalisms—indeed, they evade them—and other modes of explanation, such as logic, are not equivalent to grammatical formulations. However, insofar as we might like to bring the ineffable into closer scrutiny and control, language is a remarkable human system that proves enabling. The therapies that cry out against the need to do this are many. We might wonder, however, if they are less rather than more human in so choosing. Love may be enough for a good deal in life, but it does not conquer all; whereas language provides a system to encompass our experiences with a wide and startlingly generative and creative potential for describing a comprehensive array of experiences. Even linguists who ask each other for intuitions about grammaticality must be arriving at their intuitions mentally. The appreciation of the forms must be mental (see Katz & Bever, 1976), and grammar must be psychological. This is so even though grammarians study texts and not people.

Monkey Sees—Monkey Does

This survey did not lead to the discovery of qualitative differences between man and other species. Those who find satisfaction in this failure will insist that this is the simple truth of the matter. There is both mental and anatomical continuity from one species to another; all differences are quantitative. It is also possible, however, that the inability to find more radical differences is revelatory not of the genuine lack of such differences but of simple ignorance. I do not think the latter view can be dismissed at this time, and in this sense, I may be in closer accord with the humanist. Even on those occasions when my intuitions outbid my logic, and "I" insist that man is unique, I cannot accept the arrogance that believes it knows in what the uniqueness consists.

—David Premack, 1976, p. 560.

It is not really necessary in a book concerned with the application of linguistics to psychotherapy to wander into the issue of language in infrahuman species. However, the path has been set down throughout the years that scientists have been attempting to demonstrate the correspondences in intelligence and even linguistic performance between lower species and man. The argument is and has been replete with ambivalence. It runs along a somewhat similar line to the argument in the Bible which alternately places man a little lower than the angels, on the one hand, and as emerging from dust, on the other—to which he inevitably returns. Similarly, a historical view of man has sought to place him "within nature" as a part of natural order without too much in the way of distinguishing features, whereas at the other pole, man is described as the master of nature and discontinuous from that which is around him, both mineral and organic.

As previously stated, Darwin's major contribution, which dominated the second half of the nineteenth and twentieth centuries, was an intellectual and scientific movement that placed man in continuity with his cousins in the animal kingdom. Such sciences as comparative anatomy and embryology only served to emphasize man's continuity. Many important discoveries resulted from this vision, the outcome of which was a major advance in biological sciences. We ought to be thankful for such a change because of its heuristic value. However, it sometimes offered simplifications that led to difficult ethical problems of how man qua man treated other men. It is at this level that we come to the important issues that concern us as therapists, because we deal with human ills in the context of social and psychological systems rather than as a part of a larger biological order.

A science such as eugenics and attempts to breed human beings under Fascist regimes could probably not come about without an intellectual base that said there are, indeed, continuities in nature with superior and inferior forms forced to intermingle. On the other hand, there is a grand tradition of animal experimentation in the medical sciences which has been utilized to the betterment of man and is directed toward finding animal models for disease, animal models for conflict, and even animal models that purport to be analogues of the psychosomatic disorders and *anxiety states*. Cautionary notes are always provided by those who know that the continuities are only partial, and some students of animal behavior (Tobach & Schneirla, 1969) warned that the analogies should only be made given certain provisos concerning the differences between and among species.

One of the most intriguing temptations in the investigations of animal behavior came about in the study of our closest primate neighbors, the apes. There are also a number of experiments concerning pigtail and bonnet macacques (Kaufman & Rosenbloom, 1969; Kaufman, 1976) which suggest that analogue states to depression may be seen after mother–infant separation with associated physiological concomitants and comparable behavioral states. Other experiments concerning the bases of attachment behaviors and their relationships to later social behaviors (Harlow, Plubell, & Beysinger, 1973; Schneirla & Rosenblatt, 1961) are but a few of the fruitful areas originating in studies of simian behavior. According to his or her prior conviction, the reader may either take heart or be dismayed by a recent journal report entitled, "Monkey Psychiatrist" (Suomi, Harlow, & McKinney, 1972), that tells the story of rapid results in the social rehabilitation of 6-month-old isolate monkeys treated by 3-month-old "peers." Former failure by use of many measures was reversed in but 6 months by the exposure to nonaggressive, even clinging, younger peers. The emergence of play, grooming, and social activity, replacing self-clasping, rocking, and autisticlike behaviors, suggested to the authors that the nonthreatening stance of the therapist without fee was analogous to the psychotherapist of humans. But shared similarities are not homologies. Moreover, these "therapists" used no interpretation and no code that, by any stretch of the imagination, could be called *a language*. This may be one of those instances in which "love" may have been enough and where analysis of the transference was superfluous.

As far back as Jonathan Swift in the pre-Darwinian eighteenth century, physical and physiognomic similarities of monkeys and apes to man were recorded with the implication—yea, suggestion—that, if they looked so much like us, why could they not act as humans do? Indeed, the scene of monkeys typing away and by chance putting together a volume of Shakespeare is one example of a parody on the quasiscientific hope that humans are "nothing special." The same idea came home to me very clearly one day, as I was off to lecture, when my 3-year-old daughter asked me what I was going to talk about. I told her I was going to tell other doctors how children learn to speak. She responded with some disdain indicating, "What's so hard about that? A mommy talks and then the child just says what she says and they know how to speak." Were it as obvious as that, there would be no question in anybody's mind that if monkey sees, monkey, too, ought to be able to do. Monkeys are said to be great mimics, and they certainly have the gestural capacity to copy what humans present as a model. Why then don't they use language?

There is a long history of noble experiments in the attempt to do just that; namely, teach simians to speak. The earliest recorded attempts began in 1932 with Jacobsen, Jacobsen, and Yoshioka (Kellogg, 1968), who tried to teach Alpha, a female chimpanzee, beginning when she was a few days of age, for a period of one year. In 1932, Kellogg and Kellogg (1968) attempted to teach a female chimp, Gua, from the age of 7½ months for 9 months. She was reared at home along with one child as a control. In 1935, Kohts attempted to teach a male chimp, Joni, beginning at 1½ years for 2½ years, again with a child as a control. Finch took a 3-day-old chimp called Fin and taught him for 3 years with 2 children as controls. From 1951 to 1954, Hayes and Hayes wrote a series of reports on Viki, to whom they had taught speech, from 3 days of age for 6½ years.

All these investigators used verbal speech. All were able to elicit the typical chimpanzee noises, such as the food bark, the "o-o" cry, and screeching or screaming. However, there was very little success at formed speech. Gua, the Kellogg's chimp, was able to achieve a number of behavioral patterns which could be interpreted. The Hayes's taught Viki to say "momma" by manipulating her lips. Kellogg (1968) reported that "momma," "poppa," "cup" and possibly "up" represent the acme of chimpanzee achievement in the production of human speech sounds. The words were learned only with the greatest of difficulty, and even after the animal could reproduce them, the words were sometimes confused and used incorrectly. Many of the authors who raised chimpanzees with their own children in the earliest months remarked on the superiority of the chimpanzee to the human infant up until about 4 months. But this superiority was largely centered about the chimpanzee's motor agility. Because these authors suggested that perhaps the vocal anatomy of the chimpanzee was not suited for speech and that the animals seemed capable of some degree of comprehension to present through gestures bodily needs and other matters, subsequent authors turned to gestural representation in their experiments with simians.

Gardner and Gardner (1969, 1975) began to teach Washoe (who was not a home-raised chimp) American Sign Language (ASL), from about the age of 9 months. Their achievements led to a furor among those interested in language and especially those who claimed that man's uniqueness lay in his capacity to manipulate words. Obviously, they were correct in choosing gestural language as a more appropriate modality for the transmission of humanlike codes. Moreover, their efforts coincided with a period of controversy in linguistics when many linguists, under Chomsky's influence, proclaimed that significant evidence existed to prove that language in human beings was innate and unique.

Since June, 1966, Washoe lived in a fully furnished house trailer with access to many toys and equipment and was addressed in sign language only, without accompanying speech. She was reported being capable of 19 signs in a reliable manner after 16 months. At 36 months, Washoe seemed to be at the same stage as a child with a mean length of utterance between 1.68 and 2.06. In fact, the stage structures were compared, and it was found that she had operations of reference such as nomination (*that* + a noun), notice (*hi* + a noun), recurrence (*more* + a noun), and nonexistence (*all gone* + a noun). She could also strike relations using attributives such as big-train, possessives such as Adam-checker, locatives such as book-table, agent–action such as Adam-put, agent–object such as mommy-lunch, and action–object such as hit-ball.

She was also reported to have combined three signs; for example, "Hurry, gimme toothbrush" with an emphasizer. She used specifiers, "Open key clean" or "Key open food," and names and pronouns, "You out go" or "Roger, Washoe tickle."

At about the same time as Washoe was learning American Sign Language, David Premack (1971, 1976) was teaching his chimp, Sara, to use a set of magnetic tabs with varying symbols to represent objects in the world; for example, a blue triangle stood for an apple. Although Premack was interested in demonstrating Sara's capacity to represent, he was more concerned with revealing her capacity for certain mechanisms of intelligence as preconditions for language. For example, he tested Sara for such capacities as causal inference, representational ability, memory, second-order relations, categorical discrimination of speech sounds, and intermodal association. In one of his more intriguing experiments, he set up two disks, representing certain items, and then asked Sara to insert a disk representing the concept *the same* or *different*. In another experiment, he set up what he considered *if-then propositions*, using direct iconic representations rather than arbitrary signifiers. For example, he presented an image for a whole apple and a cut apple and then had the chimp place between them one of a number of possible agents that might produce the cut state, in this instance a knife. A dry sponge was set up with a space between it and a wet sponge, and the animal was expected to put a representation of water between. He also found that the chimp was not only able to apply her skill and knowledge to familiar object–implement pairs, but also was able to perform correctly on pairs whose states were never experienced; for example, an apple and an an apple with writing on it, or writing paper and writing paper that was wet. Premack suggested that these were not iconic but required the application of analogue processes to depict cause/effect relationships that animals were capable of representing.

Representational capacity was demonstrated by using abstract shapes for objects in the world which did not share any attributes with the signified object; as noted before, an apple was represented by a blue plastic triangle. The chimpanzee was then able to show the examiner that the apple representer was red, round, and stemmed. The experiments revealed that chimps possess a cognitive map of their world and are able to locate hidden objects. Although Premack emerged from his work somewhat optimistic that chimps can go far with their activities and that their knowledge was more than generalization, the evidence for second-order relations in primates was slight. Chimps seem to be capable of such comparisons as same–different, name of–color of–then, etc., but are not self-reflective and provide no criterial evidence that we would consider sufficient to ascribe humanness to them.

There were times when the examiners verbalized what they were doing while training the chimpanzee to recognize and associate the disks with certain things. The chimps overheard what they were being trained to grasp visually so that, when given a number of fruits to choose, merely saying the word was sufficient, at times, to have the animal make the correct choice at a level significantly above chance (Premack, 1976, p. 559). Premack felt that the differences between human and chimp intelligences were quantitative and that whatever qualitative differences we suggest from our human positions reflect instead our arrogance rather than our certainty.

Another set of experiements were carried out by Rumbaugh (Rumbaugh, Gill, & Von Glaserfeld, 1974; Rumbaugh, Von Glaserfeld, Warner, Pisani, & Gill, 1974; Rumbaugh & Gill, 1976) at the Yerkes Regional Primate Center. Rumbaugh and his associates also bypassed the vocal-auditory channel by using a set of punch keys in a computer console placed in a cage with their chimpanzee, Lana, who was slightly over two years of age when her training was begun. Rumbaugh claimed that, from his studies, apes seem able to build vocabularies above 200 words. He also claimed "only when the subject productively uses a word in novel interaction with other words syntactically is there evidence that it has a conceptual meaning." Lana was taught using a reward reinforcement technique to manipulate the 75-key console of symbols that represented varying things in the world. Each key, called a *lexigram*, had a background color to designate classes of words, whereas different geometric patterns designated specific words. The key positions were changed to obviate this clue to "meaning." Rumbaugh commented that Washoe transferred the use of the sign for "open," using it in a variety of situations where open was appropriate. Similarly, Lana was able to transfer names and colors from her training circumstances to a wide variety of novel objects and pictures. In one instance, she punched into the computer that she wished an "apple which is orange" when requesting an orange since she had no such word for the fruit. On yet another occasion, she asked for "coke which is orange," to get an orange soda. Thus, she was able to transfer and manipulate the words in her general vocabulary in novel and productive manners.

Rumbaugh and his associates listed an impressive group of words, including autonomous actors, ingestables, drinkables, and transferrable items such as balls and blankets; fixtures such as doors and body parts; pronouns such as you and this; semantic indicators such as the name of activities like drink, eat, swing, and tickle; prepositions such as behind, in into, on, out, and of; as well as colors and states. Identities and differences were marked by specific token buttons on the console; attributives were also represented, and markers were used to indicate questions. Indeed, one of the most impressive narratives concerned a series of conversations between Lana and Tim Gill on June 11, 1975, in which the examiner tried to fool the animal. Lana did not accept the trick and instead made corrective suggestions.

Rumbaugh and Gill concluded "that the findings of eight language studies served to encourage the redefinition of language in terms of an evolutionary comparative perspective which emphasizes the psychological process which underlies the public transmission of a language type of communication" (p. 576). These successes encouraged further research by some of the same investigators and others, too. Since the Gardner's experience with Washoe was with an older chimp, they decided to teach two new chimpanzees immediately after birth. Both Moja and Pili started to make recognizable signs when they were about 3 months old (Gardner & Gardner, 1975, p. 753). Moja's first 4 signs were "come," "gimme," "more," "drink," and "here," during her thirteenth week of life, and Pili's during the fourteenth week of life were "drink," "come," "gimme," "more," and "tickle." At six months, Moja had 15 signs and Pili, 13 signs. Another report by Fouts (1973) suggested that the infant female chimp Salome used the sign for food during her fourth month. The Gardners considered the exposure of their subjects to fluent Manual Sign Language (MSL) from birth as a salutary beginning for the continuation of their study. Current studies are also in progress with a chimp called Nim, who has, at last report, collected 300 signs.

From this brief review of the literature concerning attempts to teach language to chimpanzees, we apparently have to accept that these close biological neighbors to man are indeed capable of a good deal more in the way of languagelike behavior than we ever thought. However, some of the most cogent criticism of this work in designating it as a language comes from Bronowski and Bellugi (1970). They claim that there are essentially five features of language to be considered and queried with regard to chimp languages: (1) Is there a delay between the arrival of a stimulus and the utterance of a message? (2) Can the animal separate affect from content of the instruction which the message carries? (3) Is there a prolongation of reference and the ability of the message to refer backward and forward? (4) Is there an internalization of language as an instrument of reflection in which the speaker may be able to build even hypothetical messages? and (5) Is there evidence of structural reconstitution such as analysis and synthesis? Items 1 through 4 involve a clear disengagement from the immediate context. The fifth item suggests a need for a logical ability to influence the environment by understanding.

Insofar as Washoe was unable to carry messages at a distance from the immediate stimuli, she is very much like the human child showing the difficulty in separation of affect from content. For example, what she had to say referred very closely to immediate situational needs and desires, and, at times, she was able to show that certain things were not the objects of her needs. However, even three-year-old children, with average language abilities, are able to discuss matters which took place in the past, using such tense markers as "She fed him" rather than a current need being expressed. The possibility for prolongation of reference is also evidenced in the speech of three-year-old humans. These children are able to use markers which carry action from the past into the future by forming the present progressive tense ending,"-ing." Washoe was only capable of carrying out a number of extended presences indicating, for example, that she wanted *"more* cookie" or *all gone* juice."

The internalization of the language as an instrument of reflection is already evident in 2½-year-old children, who play with their words prior to going to bed (cf. Weir, 1964) and carry out syntactic play prior to sleep, even when no one is around. Psychotherapists recognize the close analogy of such behaviors to the presleep attachment of children to transitional objects which are said by Winnicott (1953) to be the precursors to the illusory realm of thinking. It is this area of performance that is most highly distinguishing when a chimpanzee is compared to a child, because it is this gradual development of inner speech (evidenced by speech while alone), that characterizes the beginnings of the use of language as a self-cueing device. This becomes even more evident if we examine a series of experiments carried out by Luria and his colleagues (1961) on the use of speech in the service of regulation of behavior that marks the gradual development of inner speech. Luria and his colleagues designed a careful procedure in which a number of visual cues were presented to children between 3 and 5 years at varying stages. The subjects were requested to respond by squeezing a rubber bulb connected to a pressure gauge attached to an automatic pressure-recording device. When the anticipation was high, the child of 3 was not able to inhibit his response. Only later were the responses able to be delayed when requested, but the delay was accompanied by *sotto voce* accompaniments, such as "wait" or "now," etc., as though thinking aloud was a transition to inner speech for behavioral regulation.

Bronowski and Bellugi's fifth point is perhaps the most important area in which Washoe fails among the requirements that would be criterial for having her productions qualify as a full-fledged language. These are the requirements for the stringing together of words into sentences. Brown (1973) writes "sign and sequence suggest grammar and so it was a momentous day when Washoe began to produce them. For grammar heretofore has been an exclusively human preserve" (p. 212). The general structural requirements of language were not fulfilled completely by Washoe. In human language, word order signifies variants of meaning, even at the two-word level. For example, a rudimentary sentence, such as "Dog bite," differs quite clearly from "Bite dog." When carried further into sentences that employ the passive voice, such as "The cat was bitten by the dog," we have an entirely different meaning than when rendered as an active sentence preserving the same order of nouns "The cat bit the dog." Thus, significance is indicated by word order as well as the specific words used. Even though Washoe did string together a number of words, there was frequent mixing of subject and object, and the word order was somewhat arbitrary.

A second locus of difference concerns the verbal rendering of demands, negations, and queries. There was no particular evidence that Washoe was able to ask for something, using a question form, or that she was capable of negating anything. On the other hand, Rumbaugh and Premack's animals were certainly able not only to ask for something but to ask for something that is out of sight, which suggests a cognitive map. Yet a third distinction concerns the problem of deixis. Functional deixis permits the same individual to be referred to as *I, me, you,* or even *he,* in accordance with altering the points in the semantic reference. Other deictic relationships are seen in the words *here* and *there,* and *that* and *this,* as signifiers for the same object according to its spatial and referential positions. There was no evidence that any of the chimpanzees were able to use these substitutive tokens. Indeed, pronominal representation was difficult for all chimps, and they were not able to use such proforms as are used in *who* questions, that is, substitutions of *who* for someone's name.

The last order of difficulty concerns the issue of category organization by inflection. It is via word endings and varieties of inflection that we are able to talk about various selections which carry references to tense, time, and pluralization. Even children who make grammatical errors based on overgeneralization and say "It breaked" instead of "It broke" are carrying out grammatical inflections which the chimpanzees were not able to master. Indeed, Bronowski and Bellugi (1970) suggested that we may only talk of an utterance as a sentence if predication is possible; inflection is the most linguistic way of analyzing the environment into parts. They went on to say that "what language expresses specifically in this scheme is the reification by the human mind of its experience that is an analysis into parts (including actions and properties) which as concepts can be manipulated as if they were objects" (p. 673).

Thus, although the semantic and cognitive accomplishments of all the trained chimpanzees were great, a difference does remain between the languages taught and achieved and the natural languages of human beings when viewed from the vantage point of formal analysis. Healy (1973) also applauded the achievements of chimp language but noted that an essential design feature of human language remained absent from chimp language and made it relatively inflexible. She suggested that the phonemic structure of human language is what permits maximal flexibility and uniqueness. The reader should recognize in this argument a variant of Hockett's (1958) discussion about the virtues of duality of patterning that makes parsimonious use of a few phonemes, permitting the user to synthesize these small units into a larger array of meaning carrying units and word parts, prefixes, etc. For example, 's for possessives and s for plurals signal different meanings but employ the same sound. Healy (1973) noted that the Gardners argued that American Sign Language was, in a sense, phonemic and could be broken into sign equivalents called "cheremes." However, she suggested that these movement variants are closer to the distinctive features that characterize articulation than a fixed set of 30 or 40 phonemes that combine to make new words. Without a phonemic structure for chimp language, much of the quality of human language was lost.

Significantly, no chimp showed any signs of self-reflection and self-awareness. There was no evidence of self-representation, nor did any chimp, once taught the language, try to teach it to another chimpanzee and carry on what would amount to a linguistic tradition. In a recent report (Rumbaugh, Rumbaugh, & Boysen, 1978), two laboratory trained chimps used their console to communicate with each other and to convey information accurately that could not have been transmitted otherwise. However, Rumbaugh and Rumbaugh (1978) cautioned against the simplistic view that the ASL sign, the token, or the lexigram had easy status as *words*. They noted the failure, in most of the studies reviewed, to distinguish the performative, here-and-now, associative status of these various signs from the symbols. Only with difficulty and special training procedure were they able to demonstrate, in a few instances, that their chimps could use the signs provided with consistent accuracy free of set contexts. In this sense, rapid concentration on the demonstration of syntactic competence was premature when referential status was in question.

Although we still stand alone as language purveyors and users, we may not be as far apart from our nearest hominid neighbor as we used to think. Unless we consider psychotherapy a nonverbal exercise, as in the case of the peer monkey described earlier, we must again turn to language. Insofar as psychotherapies, as we know them, are highly dependent on the transmission of verbal traces, we can rest assured that our study of language will take us to a sector of behavior that still involves a very special capacity in human beings. A capacity for reference, a designation by words, and a pointing without the referent being present are all central to therapists in their understanding of the linguistic productions of patients. Were patients not capable of such transmission of fantasies and events in words and in sentences, psychotherapy would not be possible.

Syntax and the Form of Language at Clinic

Sentences, not words are the essence of speech, just as equations and fractions, and not bare numbers, are the real meat of mathematics.

—Benjamin L. Whorf, 1962, p. 258.

Syntax refers to the structural order of language. As mentioned previously, Morris (1964) suggested that syntactic study concerns the relationship of sign-to-sign and that this aspect of language may be studied independently. Indeed, ever since Chomsky (1957) and the new grammarians took hold of the linguistic sciences, the scope of their efforts has been narrowed to the study of the formal relationships in syntax. The central arguments generated around this theme will be reviewed for a clear understanding prior to the application of syntactic models to the clinical issues to be considered.

When Saussure distinguished between *la langue* and *la langage* (language and speech), he sought to make a distinction between the formal aspects of language and the specific performance of each language which employs a specific set of phonemic units that constitutes speech. Recognizing, as Sapir (1921) did, that, in the first instance, language is auditory or at least auditorily organized in sound sequences, we still cannot claim this proposition valid or heuristic as a general principle for proceeding to an overriding theory of syntax; that is, linguistic ordering does not necessarily take place only through the registration of organized sound sequences. It is clear, for example, that deaf individuals can order their world and create a syntax of their representational universe in an ordered manner without benefit of sound. Moreover, no matter what language a child learns to speak, with whatever phonemic base, whether it is a Romance, a Germanic, or an Indian language, he can, by the age of 3, generally string together three to five words to represent a coherent set of relationships he wishes to express. In the beginning, these relationships are rather narrow but adequate for day-to-day communication and for negotiating most jobs with which the individual must deal. Indeed, to function in the world, we rarely need much more than the actor–action–object form to express our needs, wishes, and deeds. From Chapter 4, the reader will remember that apes can be taught to order their new words but that they lapse from their strict application of orderliness thereby confounding meaning. In addition, since their system is not phonemic, they lack flexibility to establish relational aspects of representation by inflection.

Lenneberg (1967) and others looked at syntax as a universal feature of man's innate biological endowment and potential which is in every individual born to an average expectable environment. Lenneberg's arguments, which substantiate his claim of innateness, are derived from the emergence of linguistic landmarks in close correlation with other biologically based maturational sequences, including anatomical, physiological, and motor landmarks that emerge in relation to linguistic landmarks. Indeed, the relative difficulty in suppressing language and the inability to teach language as we know it to other species are well known. The universals of semanticity, syntactic arrangement, use of vocal auditory channels, and duality of patterning all suggest a common biologic substructure.

Syntactic completeness of language also fits into the neurophysiological speculations of Lashley (1951), who suggested that in any analysis of complex behavior, from walking to speaking, we ultimately have to deal with the neural bases for serial order in behavior. At this time, we do not know how the development of syntax interacts with the development of neural order, but we do know we cannot study language without syntax if we are to consider that which is uniquely human in man's communicational system.

Perhaps because Chomsky's area of investigation was discourse analysis, he arrived at the simplifying assumptions that characterized his *transformational grammar*. Zelig Harris, his teacher, had prompted the interest in finding similarities in meanings of sentences despite varied syntactic surface arrangement. Chomsky arrived at the concept of competence as an enabling postulate which freed linguists to study sentences as objects of grammatical intuition. Linguists study languages in the form of sentences that are not uttered or cluttered by intonation or other paralinguistic encumbrances. Their purpose is to derive a minimal set of rules that could be used as a basis for any sentence generated in a language rather than studying any particular performance of that language. Thus, the rules that govern morphophonemic structures are taken for granted as defining semantic markers which, when rendered in groups, form sentences that become meaningful by the application of syntactic organizations. This model permits a complex set of structures that may be looked at under the recent rubric of transformational grammar. Indeed, transformational grammar has occupied the minds of linguists from 1957 well into the last ten years when a shift occurred from the more rigorous restrictions and demands of that discipline.

Initially, grammarians hoped that one could derive semantics from syntax and that the minimum set of rules for the analysis of phrase structures and transformation would also be the minimal set of base features by which human syntactic competence and comprehension would emerge. Once grammarians discovered these presumed rules of structuralizing language, they would have a key to the logic of language, which is every speaker's birthright.

Of course, one of the curious things about this approach to syntax is that not everyone knows how to parse a sentence or can describe to another individual what is the subject of a sentence, or the object, or the predicate adjective. But we are all able with some degree of intuition to sense grammaticality, whether it is our own or others. This must be based on some neuroperceptual and cognitive base operative in the human psyche. When one says or presumes that *it is at work*, we do not know *where it lies* or *what its constituents may be.* However, we can describe the method of linguists in analyzing sentences apart from human environments and context of expression to determine the kind of minimum apparatus necessary to generate such sentences. In that sense, the linguist works almost as the mathematician does, constructing the most parsimonious set of rules necessary to describe any *possible* sentence as well as the variety of problems that would come about when sentences are difficult to analyze because they are ambiguous or anomalous.

At this point, let me distinguish among grammar as a logical structural study, the substrate which enables such possibilities, and the self-conscious awareness of how these organizations are constituted. Almost as Freud suggested in his analysis of drives into sources, aims, and objects, we may distinguish among the three terrains. The substrate is studied by other methods—neurophysiology, anatomy, etc. The closest we may come to grammatical behavior in relation to substrate would be in hemispheric correlate studies or performance variables that are related to brain damage. Self-conscious grammatical knowledge required to parse sentences is a learned skill that characterizes certain grammarians, sixth-grade English students, and pedants. Grammar as a structural study is the focus of the transformationalists. The capacity to string signs (words) into a given set of relationships that the human psyche has at its disposal to encode and decode its thoughts and experiences may be represented by an example: A simple declarative sentence, *John hit the ball,* may be looked at as a paradigm from which the individual may derive a number of other sentences, such as the negative, *John does not hit the ball,* or the passive voice, *The ball was hit by John,* the imperative, *John, hit the ball!,* and the interogative, *Did John hit the ball?*

Chomsky's original formulation of transformational grammar took the position that every surface form of a sentence or *surface structure* could be seen as a variant of an abstract *deep structure* which is then acted on by a transformational rule. The latter rule, along with specific lexical items that are inserted into appropriate slots, will determine the surface appearance of a sentence. Moreover, identity of meaning can then be derived from synonomy of deep structure. Thus, the active and passive forms reduce to identical deep structures which render them identical in meaning. Ambiguity derives from a surface structure having at least two possible deep structures, and anomaly derives from senselessness. Thus, meaning was thought to reside in the interplay of phonemic structure and deep grammatical structure. For example, in

    (1)   Flying planes can be dangerous.
    (2)   They are eating apples.

sentences (1) and (2) each have two alternative deep structural interpretations and are therefore ambiguous. Sentence (1) may offer a deep structural interpretation which corresponds to:

    (3)   Planes that fly can be dangerous (whereas grounded planes are not).

or

    (4)   The flying of planes can be dangerous.

They are eating apples may be interpreted as:

    (5)   They are in the process of eating. What they are eating are apples.
    (6)   They are in a designative sense apples which are to be eaten.

Linguists represent these variations in tree diagrams which take the following representational form S → NP + VP (V + NP). Every sentence (S) is made up of a noun phrase (NP) plus a verb phrase (VP). The latter includes a verb (V) plus a noun phrase (NP). Sentence (2) construed as the alternative forms (5) and (6) are represented diagrammatically in Figure 1.

Later Chomskian models and some of those of his critics shifted more and more toward surface structures as mediators of meaning. In the hands of some linguists (Lakoff, 1971; McCawley, 1968; Chafe, 1970), syntax was brought to even lesser significance by the espousal of a *generative semantics*. Without getting too involved in this intramural discussion within the family of linguists, it can be said that generative semanticists believe the system can be rendered more reasonably and parsimoniously with semantics as primary rather than syntax. However, generative grammarians do not claim that all that humans take as meaningful depends only on syntactic knowledge but also on mental organizations and experiences lying adjacent to such knowledge. For example, if one were to state in the context of the political scene in the liberal northeast that Richard Nixon was the finest president in the past 25 years, it would most certainly be understood as ironic. However, to understand the irony, one must draw upon information that is not syntactic. Nevertheless, to create the irony one has to understand the simple arrangement of words in the syntactic form presented so that the proposition may be inverted in meaning for one's best reading of its significance and meaning.

In terms of the mental substrate necessary for grammar to be understood, Bruner (1974) suggested that there are innumerable, nonverbal, early childhood experiences that show similar functional organizations which are prior to grammatical knowledge and prescribe its form. He cited games, such as "give and take," and bringing closure to inter-

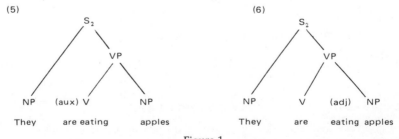

Figure 1

changes by gestural punctuation. These experiences provide structurally homologous precursors for the development of grammatical form. In these early perceptual and attentional structures, he saw formal action structures carried out toward and away from the developing self as the developmental precursors to case grammar forms, such as agent, action, object, and sentence closure. Thus, in one direction, we may move from behavioral units toward language units. We also may move back from language units toward behavioral units and, if we wish to suggest a biological base, it may be that we move from behavioral units to neuroperceptual units. The notion that attention and closure converge to form the communicative mode may be of significance in our ultimate understanding of how brain function coheres with aspects of perception and mind.

From yet another vantage point, the very form of our particular language is said to have a molding effect on our view of the world. Although the limits of naturally formed grammatical entities may be defined by biology, the proposition that each language provides a differing world has been advanced and is called the *theory of linguistic relativity*, known more generally as the *Whorf–Sapir hypothesis*. It is most often mentioned in relation to reference but also has application at the level of syntax. Linguistic relativity simply states that the world and its elements is not only coded by our language, but that the structure of our language forms our world view. The way in which we construct our sentences tells us something about our relationship to the world as well as the relationships in the world. Grammarians are somewhat uncomfortable with this proposition in its strong form because they believe that, from a competence vantage point, every language has the possibility of representing that which is present in any other language point by point. Each language simply utilizes different organizational structures provided by that language. This view must be uneasily held except as a most formal statement when we look at individual examples. Whorf (1962) described certain Indian languages in which, for example, cleaning out the barrel of a gun with a ramrod is not portrayed in a syntactic organization in which we have an actor on the gun putting a ramrod in it and doing the work. Rather, the Shawnee language "dissects nature differently" (p. 208). In the Indian sentence, to describe "clean it with a ramrod" extracts a dig space as the interior of the hole and the motion of a tool as central. Similarly, we are told that Russians are frequently late for appointments, even treaty signing, not out of any particular malice toward those whom they have invited but out of an imperfect representation of aspects of time in their language (cf. Wilson, 1978). McNeill and McNeill (1967) have also described the generation of negative forms within the Japanese language, indicating that there are four modes of negation, each with its own word and position. One form pertains to nonexistence, one to the negation of a proposition, another to a denial of a wish, etc. It may be for this reason that an Oriental, whose knowledge of English is imperfect, may say "Yes" when the proper intended English translation may be "No." For example, if you present an Oriental who is used to his own language with the negative query "Mrs. Smith is not at home?", he might say "Yes" because he agrees with what you have said, not because he wants to say "On the contrary, she is at home rather than not at home."

Such behavioral alterations, based on syntactic rules, may not enter into the formal analysis which would permit an individual to understand the nature of the rule structure of a particular grammar that has been the province of certain linguists in the past years but would certainly be helpful to us in getting along with people of different language backgrounds. The "mathematics of grammar" is a reasonable academic enterprise. The development of grammar is even a practical enterprise for studying developing children, using their capacity to produce and understand more complex utterances as a measure of cognitive growth. However, it should be noted that we have, in the study of grammar, but a limited scope for the analysis of all that is represented in a single linguistic act.

As psychotherapists, we tend to be much more interested in the compendium of linguistic accompaniments. On the other hand, if we ignore predication and syntax, we ignore one of the central ways that man has of analyzing his environment into parts by grouping and regrouping percepts into innumerable new arrangements. Concepts of the most varied kind become communicated by being encoded in a potentially infinite set of sentences. The notion that each symbolic expression has a natural medium for expression, because its formal characteristics cohere with that which is to be expressed, was formulated during the Renaissance in the *Paragonae*, which was later adopted by the classic German scholars Winckelmann and Lessing. The arguments offered in that treatise are expressed in the idea that each art form has an appropriate expressive vehicle more suited to it than to other vehicles. For example, sequential representations would be much better represented in forms that have a temporal, evanescent element, such as poetry and literature, whereas sculpting a sequential referent is more difficult. On the other hand, static vehicles, such as painting, really ought not try to represent movement or motion. Such examples as Marcel Duchamp's *Nude Descending a Staircase* tend to confound such arguments. The Romantic painters sought to beat the restriction by representing sequential events at the peak of their movement and excitement, inviting the observer to carry the action through to its end by extension of the depicted action.

It is interesting to consider this matter, even if restrictive, because we frequently stretch our vehicle for expression to include contents not suitable to the vehicle. *Metaphors* and *similes* are examples of such relational forms to which we will pay closer attention in Chapter 6. But syntactic problems are also evident in metaphor. A metaphor extensively studied by Rubinstein (1972) is *John is a fox.* To understand or interpret such a comment, we would have to know that a fox is sly; John is sly; John is like a fox; John is a fox. We could represent such a set of relationships as identities that could be represented in a symbolic logical form. It could also be represented as an overlapping set in a Venn diagram using a visual rather than a verbal model. Miller (1979) in his unpublished paper "Images and Models, Similes and Metaphors" argues that, to understand metaphors we are dealing with, models and not concrete images and models are lawfully defined abstract templates for words, images, or whatever.

As therapists, we depend on metaphoric representations, because so much of what is said in the course of therapy is produced in personalized reconcretizations of more abstract ideas. To decipher such productions, transformational grammar applies insofar as translation of referents into understandable units must be complemented by grammatical knowledge that includes the permissible slots into which words may be plugged. The words that are plugged into varying positions in a sentence sequence must agree with the constraints that are dictated by the rules of formal relationships. Chomsky's phrase, "colorless green ideas sleep furiously," provides an example of adequate grammatical form with words plugged into available and appropriate grammatical slots. Adjectives are placed where adjectives belong, and nouns are treated as nouns, but their choice in this sentence does not obey the rules for permissible entries because of what linguists describe as *feature analysis*. Although we may be willing to accept the statement as poetry and even to attempt to understand the negations and the dualisms and

the very unusualness of the sentence, the sentence still seems anomalous and is not meaningful without a complex process of psychic reshuffling. Poetry also draws on this aspect of feature analysis.

T. S. Eliot (1930) used such metaphysical representations in "The
Love Song of J. Alfred Prufrock" in which twilight is said to be "like a
patient etherized upon a table." We understand the grammar of that
sentence, too, but we do not easily understand the meaning unless we
can determine in what way twilight bears any relationship to a patient
etherized upon a table. E. E. Cummings (1926) made paradoxical use of
punctuation and words in order to make a particular poetic point. He
also provided a prime example of disobedience to simple syntactic dictates regarding the use of certain lexical items or phrases in sentence
slots whose formal determinants do not permit such use. For example,
"Spring is like a perhaps hand" has syntactic clarity but "a perhaps
hand" is not expectable by the rules of feature analysis as an insertion
relating to the qualities of Spring. In a simpler example,

> The window ate the stew.

the word *window* is inappropriate because the verb *ate* must have a noun
agreement among the features that describe the noun, which include
animate and capable of oral activity; *window* does not agree with these
lexical requirements.

To summarize, transformational grammar is made up of a hypothetical abstract deep structure acted upon by transformational rules in combination with phrase structure rules and lexicons that are permissible by
the potential sentence's formal restraint on permissible features. The
final result is a specific sentence with a specific surface structure.

If we are determined to look for syntactic ordering devices within
our clinical psychological theory of mind, I would point to Freud, who,
although not specifically interested in grammar, did have a tacit
grammar in his system. This may come as a surprise to some, because
Freud seemed so disinterested in such formalism in his writing. But, in
his energic theory, he suggested that there is a difference between
primary-process and secondary-process discharge. Although many individuals use such terms as secondary- and primary-process thinking,
the terms are inappropriate as an extension of Freud's notion. He clearly
was referring to the relative mobility of *cathexis of psychic energy* and not
to the *structure of grammar*. What he did suggest was that the mobility of
cathexis of psychic energy in primary process underlies the lack of order-

liness that one finds in the rule-governed behavior seen especially in the transformation of symbolic representations.

The secondary-process discharge, by virtue of its orderliness, could then be construed in its manifest form as bound energy manifested in grammaticality, orderliness, and structure. However, the condensations and displacements which characterized dream life, that is, the relative abundance of primary-process modes of discharge rather than secondary-process modes of discharge, dispose dreams to show greater symbolic ambiguity than that found in overt verbal grammar. One can think of the background against which dreams are formed: Freud insisted that it was a "dream thought" that was somehow repressed during the previous day and that the expression of the dream thought in a manifest dream was the result of the complex action of dream work which then led to the particular form of representation in a largely visual percept called *a dream*. Interestingly enough, the syntax was already thought to be there insofar as the dream thought had to be ordered in some sense. The syntactic ordering, prior to expression, is disguised by the action of a censor and by the rendering in a nonverbal vehicle (as a percept) in a dream. Edelson (1972, 1976) made the most extensive attempt to integrate the theories of Chomsky and Freud, especially in regard to the interpretation of dreams. Chomsky's earliest form of transformational grammar, in which meaning resides in deep structure, has maximum affinity to Freud's theory of dream formation and the interpretative process in general but excludes dynamic, defensive considerations.

The second place in which Freud dealt with grammar, without expressly mentioning it, concerned the organization of drive representations. Although he believed that conflict emerged between id impulses and superego prohibitions which led to ego activity, such as defense and inhibition, he also sought the origin of wishes in the theory of drives. Thus, he postulated that one can look at a drive as having a source, an aim, and an object. The source is to be studied physiologically as "the work that the body causes the mind to do." In that sense, it is a motivational core which is at the interface between biology and psychology. However, the particular form that a drive takes is as a wish. Wishes must have structures—they are vectorial. The structure is usually "I want to" or "I wish to" or "I should like to," according to how much organization and understanding is available with respect to immediate future and present gratification. The aim is described as passive or active. The object is the element that is most determined by the layering of experience. The simplest form of a wish is "I wish *to do* or *have done to me* something by *this* or *that* person." A grammatical form is implied. In this sense, a grammatical structure must be considered as a part of any motivational psychology.[1] The developmental matter of when such wishes come into being, in what form, with what objects, and what aims is a problem of representational propensities at varying developmental stages. The fact that wishes are tacitly considered in formal representations is an issue that overlaps the understanding of grammatical form.

Clinically, we deal with wishes as idiosyncratic representations that arise at varying stages of development, whose residues may help us to understand what the phase specific demands and what the compromises were like. However, the capacity for form is a factor that ought to give us some clue to the relathionship of wants derived from biological sources and wishes characterized as varying verbal traces. There is an old argument among linguists as to whether or not single word utterances are "holophrastic," that is, when the child says one word does he mean a whole sentence? Argument has been made that *holophrasis* means grammatical knowledge rather than psychological need expression, which implies expression and expectation of satisfaction sequences. The limited capacity for representation, seen in the curtailment of the expression, is a constraint on verbalization not intent. At present, the argument seems to be settled that grammar is "potential" in average developing individuals, but that single word utterances do not represent grammatical knowledge, although they may imply wish fulfillment. On the other hand, the wish structure of children is clearly evident in the appeal function that expressive vocalization evinces in the caretaking environment. Sapir (1921) suggested that, in the beginning, children do not demand, but that parents ascribe an appeal function which then determines that what originally is an expressive cry, and then a single word, be treated as though it were a sentence demanding action. In that sense, it is not the drive expression from within but the ministration from without that determines the particular organization of how needs are expressed. These responses may be by accident of whoever is parenting as well as of necessity.

One would wonder whether or not syntax would be a useful in-

---

[1]This should be qualified for simple $S \rightarrow R$ systems in which mediating processes are not presumed. These may be seen as organismic responsiveness models.

strument for clinical observation. If one accepts a recent review of the literature by Maher (1972) concerning linguistic factors in schizophrenia, one finds a surprising conclusion that syntactic factors do not seem to be as relevant as one would have expected. Indeed, with the exception of *word salad* and *verbigeration* (forms of linguistic production seen during acute phases of schizophrenia), we find very little in the organization of syntactic structure of psychotics that could be described as uniquely psychotic language. Apparently, grammar once "learned," just as mathematical structures once learned, is a remarkably stable organizational feature of the human mind. This notion could be used as another organizational reason to suggest that autonomous ego functions may indeed by highly separable from motivational, conflict-ridden difficulties.

One does find some evidence of difficulty, however, in the development of language-delayed children. Childhood schizophrenics and autistic children show some disorders in syntax, either as complete disorganizations for transient periods of time or over longer periods of time (Shapiro, Huebner, & Campbell, 1974). This area will be examined in Chapter 11.

Cloze techniques also reveal that schizophrenics are more likely to use unusual words in their consecutive productions than would normals. Salzinger, Portnoy, and Feldman (1964) showed the unusual use of lexical items in sentences by schizophrenics. Andreason and Pfohl (1976) collapsed grammar and thought using language as the empirical indicator of thought and recently examined schizophrenics' productions and compared them to manics' utterances. They found no characteristic differences. Children with developmental language disabilities show difficulty in sequencing and comprehension of complex grammatical forms as part of their learning disorders. Freedman and Steingart (1975) suggested that depressive individuals are much more likely to have simple narrative sentences and less hierarchical complexity of syntax than other individuals. They analyzed the linguistic productions of individuals according to code, status, and focus. *Code* refers to the hierarchical complexity of syntax expressed as fragmented language, simple and extended narrative language, complex portrayal, and complex condition language. *Status* refers to whether there is self or object representation or interaction between the two. Their analysis of 10-minute samples of a paranoid individual suggested a larger number of uses of conditional language, whereas the depressed individual showed more instances of narrative language consonant with the rest of his inhibited behavior.

Aside from these more formal studies, perhaps the most relevant area that psychotherapists focus on in syntactic performance concerns the nuances of behavior that appear as formal rigidities or tendencies of patients with particular character structures. Just as one may take a fingerprint to distinguish one individual from another on biological grounds, individual tendencies do express ideas and attitudes that may be considered a feature of style. Rosen (1977) wrote extensively about the analysis of style and, before his death, began to describe a series of difficulties in reference in individuals who exhibit certain character styles. These usage propensities could be the earmark of diagnostic aids which we may tacitly use. If they could be put in the form of more systematic statements utilizing an understanding of syntax, we may have a handy index to character. There are individuals, for example, who constantly express themselves in the passive voice as though they did not ever carry out any action on or against others, but merely are carried along by a world which acts on them. If one takes Fenichel's (1941) idea that one of the jobs of analysis (and any therapy) is to turn the victim into an actor and a participant in his own life, then individuals who speak in the passive voice will at sometime during therapy have to be confronted with the fact that they look upon themselves as continuously being carried along by the flow of some outside force.

For example, individuals who, during therapy, constantly say "It occurs to me that my thoughts are leading me to the following conclusion," might, in yet another instance, say "Your tone of voice *makes me* feel unhappy," or "Lying down *causes me to feel* excited." Any and all of these statements must be looked at as though the individual who is talking has nothing to do with what happens to him. These passive-form expressions have all the defensiveness exemplified in the statement "It's only a dream."

This is but a simple example of a sector in which habitual syntactic form may denote something about a patient that has deeper characterological significance. This topic will be treated more extensively in Chapters 7 and 10. But, by and large, there are no specific general pathologies of syntax that are not developmental or organic. The temporary disruption mentioned in schizophrenic word salad is perhaps the only exception. The illogicality of the paranoid is not a syntactic issue, and the results of the cloze technique seem to lie in the interface between syntax and reference and associational deviance.

The syntactic expressions of the therapist have not been considered extensively, but there is a recent study by Dahl, Teller, Moss, and

Trujillo (1978), using a tape-recorded analysis, which suggests that speech syntax acts as an "incidental stimulus in the communication of mental contents" which each speaker is motivated both to conceal and express. Using ten psychoanalytic interventions by the therapist, they showed countertransference attitudes as revealed in syntactic properties. To date, this is a unique study of actual interventions using syntactic analysis.

Schafer (1976) approached the interpretation of transference in a manner that has some kinship to grammatical considerations when he discussed interpretation as metaphor. In laboring to look at interpretative effects as more than "paraphrases of an already fully constituted experience" (p. 353), he suggested that the metaphor creates a new experience which the patient has not himself realized. I might add, though it is implied in Schafer's text, that what is therapeutic is that it has not been realized in words before. Words provide a vehicle which is useful for future constructive creative experience and which extricates the patient from the distortions due to past experience. Schafer further claimed that every interpretation implicitly has the structure of a simile: "This is like that." As we pursue the role of syntax, it will become increasingly obvious that formal structure yields to semantic interpretations and that the intramural battle among linguists is a natural outcome of attempts to construe the data in the most parsimonious manner for ultimate use in natural human expression.

It might seem that the central thrust of modern linguistics is not very relevant to us as therapists. However, the concordance of aspects of Chomsky's theory of transformations to aspects of Freud's theory of symbol formation cannot be denied. Grammar *per se* seems remote but cannot be dismissed in expressing relationships between both parties of a therapeutic dyad.

Reference at Clinic

Among Morris's three sectors that are appropriately studied by linguists, the problem of reference, or the relationship of words to things, is perhaps one of the most relevant areas to attract our attention as therapists. To make the bridge from the previous chapter, one must recognize that words, as units of meaning, are probably as arbitrary as are sentences, as units designed to convey the flow of relationships between thoughts. The relation of words to their smaller units— morphemes and phonemes—and to their larger units—sentences— provides us with a way of looking at the building blocks of language itself. However, analysis into units does not permit us to ask a more general question about the relationship of words to thoughts. Considering referential issues permits more formal study of the relation of the mental activity involved in forming and applying words to those elements that are registered as perceptions emanating from the external world; that is, the things of the world relative to the names by which we call those things.

Clearly, the initial sounds made by an infant have no specific reference to anything in the external world. Indeed, if we can postulate anything about the vocalizations, they are more related to states of disequilibrium which we can classify as being in the comfort–discomfort series defined by Lewis (1936) (see Chapter 3). Lewis suggested that the original comfort vocalizations are rarely nasal in phonic value and include /ga/, /ka/, /cha/, /ra/, and /na/, /ta/, /da/, and /ba/. The discomfort series are usually nasal vowel consonant combinations: /wa/, /la/, /nga/, /ha/, /ma/, and /na/. During the earliest months of infancy, these vocal accompaniments of varied, undifferentiated, affective states are likely expressions of motor overflow in an undifferentiated organism. The fact that earliest distress sounds are back sounds and nasal is a happenstance of the open-mouthed state of the infant in distress. The bilabials /b/ and /p/ involved in comfort states are likely the result of more discrete movements of the lips in quiet states and even early imitation. Certainly the throaty cooing of the responsive 3- to 4-month-old child is also associated with open-mouthed smiling.

When these early sounds become representations of things which are consensually validated in the external world, a common social designator is established in the child, and a turning point is recognized when reference is born. To follow an old model from Bühler (1934), already noted in Chapter 3 it is the move from the expressive to the appeal function which marks the dawning of conscious awareness that a particular vocalization brings a satisfaction from a dimly perceived environmental surround. Such appeals then become differentiated into distinctive vocalizations that become units of reference permitting the transmission of experiences to be shared. The sequential course of how this comes about is reflected in the question of what words stand for.

This problematic question has been answered in many ways, ranging from the simple notion that words are merely labels for things to a more comprehensive view that words carry dynamic referential impact, too, registered not only in the vocal-auditory and conceptual channels, but also in the affecto-motor systems derived from the earlier sensory motor stages and extending to later purely mental organizations. This latter view was also elaborated by Freud (1900/1953) who described thought as "trial action." Hallucinatory wish fulfillment was Freud's designation for the first representation that came to mind when the motor apparatus was not immediately engaged because of delay; that is, the mind was thought to reevoke the percept associated with the last experience of arousal and satisfaction. Those postulated hallucinations evolve into the mental traces that become associated with words. Thus, Freudian psychology prescribed that ontogenetically all thoughts are wishes and all words affective. However, just as Piagetian psychology moves away from sensory motor and synchronic responsiveness as the organism develops so we too will not be discouraged to find that thoughts become emancipated, more or less, from their wishful origins, and ideas attain a sort of life of their own. Indeed, psychoanalysts, such as Edelson (1972), take their cue from Chomsky and believe that the unconscious, like the conscious mind, is made up of abstract conceptual forms and not percepts. Lacan's unconscious is structured with similar abstractions. In maturity, then, we operate with ideas which are only more or less close to their action associates and affects.

Experiments at later developmental stages suggest that words are not simply labels but carry the dynamic association that is the remnant of earlier, sensory-motor, affective schemata. Another way to construe the matter would be to suggest that the features that define a word include an affective valence of some proportion. An ingenious set of experiments, designed by Kaden, Wapner, and Werner (1955), showed that, when a subject establishes an eye level by regulating an illuminated beam, the normative level is skewed if a heavy or light appearing item is projected instead of the neutral light beam. The subject compensates by fixing the level of the illuminated heavy object higher, and significantly lower with light-weighted items. The results are the same when illuminated printed words that have an airy light versus heavy connotation are projected instead of objects. Ingenious experiments are nice for verification, but there are also clinically important data that might verify the dynamic schematization of words. Stories are told about the use of words with roughly equivalent meanings making all the difference in their impact. Extraclinical examples of effective and ineffective journalists abound. Thus, the concept reference must include, in addition to the word–thing relationship, an additional associated referent of a potential affect which varies in degree with the word used.

As an example to convey my meaning, one need but mention an array of words which stand for human feces. The responses by auditors suggest that words have impact on persons that cannot be accounted for under the word-as-label concept. To take the matter one step further, it is clear that, insofar as the word functions as a label, it is a label which includes a bevy of associational probabilities that can be hierarchically arranged in accord with a similar hierarchy of affective responses. For example, *feces* does not stimulate much in the way of disgust or shock for most auditors and *shit* might elicit more emotive response, especially in some social settings. *Stool* offers little other than a clinical ring, but if one were asked for the word used by one's mother to designate one's bowel movement when a toddler, one could probably bring a blush to the cheeks of the most restrained among us. The latter example is an easy entrée to the problems of the development of reference and the progressive nature of word–thing association or, as we will see later, word–concept association.

Werner and Kaplan (1963) describe the mother and child as looking at the world together. The dyad gradually gains distance one from the other just as Mahler described in the separation–individuation process. The original global sensory-motor–affective apprehension of the per-ceived world is gradually differentiated into a repetitious set of auditory-vocal representations which gradually become pointed to in gesture and are then pointed to by the use of vocalizations—words. It is not just a matter of curiosity that the German word for 'pointing' *deuten* is incorporated in the German word for 'meaning' *Bedeutung*. Indeed, words certainly point to things, actions, persons, ideas, but they also stand for conceptual models. Freud's (1900/1953) original notion was that word presentations in the psychic apparatus have their parallel registration as unconscious thing–presentations (see Chapter 2) ac-cording to topographic theory. However, he did not carry his anal-ysis far enough because his scheme suggests that most of us, when we use words, have specific things in mind. Why so brilliant a mind should have skipped over what was obviously available to Ogden and Richards in the 1920s when they wrote *The Meaning of Meaning* (1923) is a puzzle. It will be less of a puzzle, however, if we consider the frame of reference that Freud was trying to advance and what he was attempting to achieve by invoking the word–thing-presentation scheme.

Ogden and Richards (1923/1946) added that words stand for concepts of class categories as well as for things. Indeed, data available from free-imagery experimentation suggest that many words do not elicit a visual representation at all. The best likely description of what we have in mind is, for example, an idealized chair—a generalization which would include all those objects on which we sit in our comfortable society. This factor of a word standing for a concept or class of objects takes us one step further up the developmental ladder away from simple representa-tion as depiction.

On the other hand, it is likely that Freud was devoted to the idea of word–thing representations because he was most interested in under-standing the regression to visual percepts in dream images. Indeed, he postulated that complex ideas, as well as words, might appear as bizarre pictorial sequences and arrangements in dreams. Dream thoughts, whose referents were ideas organized as words in a syntactic arrange-ment, were transformed into pictorial representations while asleep which could only be deciphered by a string of associations that led back again to words. As has been noted, each residue, word, and thing were thought to be segregable systematically in different portions of the hypothetical mental apparatus, obeying different rules for transformation into images that impinge on varied senses. Only in reaching conscious awareness do they appear as attached to words. Freud's genius was surely in his method which has permitted us to understand dreams rationally and thus provided therapists with a semantic based in part on reference. This method further illuminated the significance of the apparently meaningless by permitting the translation of parapraxes into meaningful units. Although his topographic theory considered these matters, his later writings did not elaborate these early themes, for he became more interested in issues of defense, transference, and structural themes than further decipherment of symbolization.

As therapists, we are all interested in looking at developmental issues that influence the sequences of referential forms. However, we are indeed more interested in this matter from the standpoint of how regressive developmental forms and modes affect verbal presentations within therapeutic settings. We use such words as "primitive" or "archaic" or "regressive" to designate a number of tendencies of form usage that we consider appropriate to certain stages of development or of altered ego states and not to others. For example, if we describe a reference as "concrete" as a feature of retardation or schizophrenia, is it really a description of the referential forms used in childhood? This would be a content regression. Werner and Kaplan (1963) stated "In reference by pointing, the object remains stuck in the concrete situation, in reference by symbolization the characteristic features of the objects are lifted out and are realized in another material medium" (p. 43). The other material media used are vocal, graphic, or pictorial modes of representation. The vehicle, of course, is the word and, at times, an icon.

When Werner and Kaplan discussed the features of objects, they introduced us to the concerns that cluster about the development of abstract functions of childhood and provide a link to a central issue within general linguistics and syntax. An example of the link was found in Chomsky's index sentence "colorless green ideas sleep furiously." Although that phrase has been studied from a grammatical standpoint in the previous chapter, let us consider it now as a problem of reference. What the sentence disobeys are the rules for feature analysis that are tacitly implied when words are lifted out from their concrete reference and realized in sentences that demand formal rigor for syntactic analysis. In order to explicate this idea, consider the sentence *The boy hits the dog with a stick.* The sentence makes sense not only with respect to the concrete realistic possibility of a boy hitting a dog with a stick, but, in a formal consideration of the sentence, the agent, the action, and the object are grammatically "well placed" as defined by the arrangement of the appropriate words in the appropriate sentence slots. If we now abstract from that sentence the subject, the verb, the object, and the indirect object, as we did in the chapter on syntax, and lay them out on a hypothetical scheme, and use them as the most abstract base into which the specific words must be plugged in, we find that some words are permissible in some positions and others are not. Indeed, given only the words in the sentence above, we can redistribute them in the following manner: *The dog hits the boy with a stick.* It may not be believable, given the nature of dogs that they could use a stick in an instrumental way. However, it would be even less believable if we rendered the sentence *The stick hit the boy with the dog.*

Both sentences obey the "nouniness" required by the sentence's noun slots but present uncertain and unlikely reference for our consideration. The sentence slot rules are also obeyed in Chomsky's sentence, but a similar intuition of unlikeliness is evoked on semantic parsing. Thus, the rules of syntax also prescribe a feature analysis for words, describing which word units have permissible referential and semantic significance so that they may be inserted within certain slots. Indeed, using the same words, an even more interesting sentence emerges that will not qualify as grammatical to any natural speaker: *The hit dog the boy stick with.* This has the ring of complete nonsense and would not be translated into imagery or external reference. Rather, the particular arrangement has the psychological impact of a jumble of words.

It is of value to attend to these examples not because they have any direct clinical significance, but to suggest that even the formalisms described under the heading of syntax and grammar are not completely removed from semantic readings of sentences and their subunits, words. The significance to dream analysis is not immediately apparent, *but* if we look at the nongrammatical arrangement as a series of images projected in the sleeping state, we have a dream. The elements of an orderly sentence are represented in an immediate nonsequential frame or in a sequential frame that demands secondary revision into phrases requiring conjunction. The orderliness to which they apply is arrived at by reshuffling and translation or interpretation into an ordered sentence by symbolic transformation.

Linguists are not much interested in the barriers to understanding that occur on dynamic grounds. However, they do consider what features render a text grammatical—translated this signifies "capable of comprehension." They do not require energic postulates to describe the effects of the mobility of cathexis of unconscious functioning; they simply refer to the rule bondedness of grammaticality that native speakers intuit naturally. Our discomfort with dreams parallels the discomfort of apprehending a poorly ordered sentence. Not understanding is not easily accepted. What is left out in this aspect of the discussion is the further discomfort of apprehending a poorly ordered sentence. Not understanding is not easily accepted. What is left out in this aspect of the discussion is the further discomfort derived from deeper infantile wishes not revealed in linguistic formalisms.

The process of the development of reference in children is intimately tied to grammar as well as to word–thing–concept relationships. Once the vocalizations of the child begin to take on referential significance and the word "mama" becomes the clear reference for the mother of a child, other words follow in rapid succession and are incorporated into a referential system of signifiers (words) that can be flexibly applied to the external world as perceived. The child moves from pointing to thinking about his world in a corpus of sound–memory traces, which are used for thinking in a code about the world and ultimately talking about that world with others, whom the child can trust to understand him when they are addressed. After all, the code as a specific dialect comes from the mother and her culture.

We have already discussed holophrasis as a syntactic concept, but its compelling force comes from experiential referential postulates, not grammatical necessity. The context of verbalization permits the adult auditing a child to infer a wish when a child speaks, and its fulfillment leads to contentment. However, there is a difference between words as signals and action provokers and speech acts that bring about the intention of a speaker and the words representing knowledge of grammatical relations.

The puzzle of trying to analyze two-word sentences according to a syntactic form, rather than the context of reference, led to disarray and even some dismay when it was discovered that performance rules were engrafted on components of competence. Although it is true that children arrange their two-word phrases right from the start in an orderly, even grammatical manner, the meaning comes not only from the sequence but from the context of expression. Bloom (1970) led the way in revealing the inadequacy of two-word grammars that ignored context. She directed her attention, as other developmental linguists did after her, toward a grammatical analysis of two-word phrases of children. Grammatical analysis of the phrase "mommy sock" was used as a case in point. Context analysis revealed that in some instances the phrase referred to "the sock belonging to mommy"; at other times it referred to a wish that the child's own sock be placed on her foot. Thus, the meaning of the phrases were better explicated when the context was explicit and available for inclusion in the analysis.

In addition to using words for wish fulfillment, children seem to enjoy simply playing with words once they are learned. In addition to taking words to bed with them in prespeech monologues, one- to two-year-old children seem to expect that their new found designations will be met by reciprocal speech from adults. Children at this stage will frequently "point and say" until a significant adult brings closure by repeating or verifying the correctness of the utterance thus making every utterance a dialogue. Words are learned in a reciprocal relationship, and social return becomes part of their meaning. Although the capacity for reference is innate, the situation of its emergence is social and reciprocal. Thus, every utterance in the code has the meaning of a social act as well as its reference to things and actions in the world. Ninio and Bruner (1978) criticized Werner and Kaplan for not providing an explanation for the shift to the comtemplative attitude and the attainment of reference as an outcome of the child's ability to understand the social rules for achieving dialogue. According the them, it is in this setting that the relationship between signified and signifier is realized. They described and analyzed the sequential behavior of a mother and a child between the ages of 8 months and 18 months who were reading a book together, and they found a constant sequence of attentional vocatives (Look!), query (What's that?), label (It's an X), and feedback utterance (Yes, laughter). The dialogue form is also obeyed with clear evidence of turn taking similar to that found by Stern, Jaffee, and Beebe (1975) in younger infants. Thus, lexical labels begin to emerge in a set dialogue form, replacing earlier reciprocal smiles, reaching, pointing, or babbling. This view places reference well within the interactional form necessary for therapy and lends some veractiy to those who would view therapy as a reexperiencing of the separation–individuation process.

Even thinking to oneself may be thought of as talking to oneself. Lewis Carroll's *Alice in Wonderland* provides a glaring example of the variety of thinking aloud that we frequently think of as a dialogue. Alice is not the only one who may be accused of such a breach of mental privacy. It is a frequent habit of many people in such circumstances as driving alone, playing tennis, and daydraming. Consider this matter in the context of the requirements of the couch monologue in psychoanalysis. In asking the patient to speak in the midst of our relative silence, we confound years of experience with the significance of language as an exchange medium. The patient must temporarily suspend the reciprocation he has come to expect as a part of the experience of language use. Indeed, lying down and not looking at one's dyad partner provides an unusual sensory deprivation, enabling projection onto an imagined other and forcing the tendency to transference distortion. That is, the imagined object of discourse is fostered because the analyst is not seen and is vocal only rarely.

These examples are not the only circumstances in which the rules of reference may be confounded by their developmental origins. The lack of distancing parallels the incomplete abstractness of use that would assure that words have only clearcut denotations or even social connotations. Frequently, we can find rules of use as well as personal referents that are idiosyncratic. In fact, we can observe patients using words in very special ways. There are patients who fall into certain diagnostic categories in which one might determine that words are not sufficiently distanced to carry out the work that we generally require of them. They seem embroiled secondarily in conflict and do not retain their relative autonomy. Rosen (1966) described a number of patients with borderline psychological organizations whose vagueness of reference revealed that they assumed the therapist understood what they were saying even though he did not use the words of the code in a usual manner. This may represent a way station to transitivism, as found in schizophrenia, in which the patient assumes that others know his thoughts because the separation of minds that we all assume is not accepted. Similarly, the closeness of the word to its original tendency to set off action is another highly significant parameter of referential confusion found in patients.

Linguists distinguish among a symbol, a sign, and a signal. A signal is an elicitor of action—the vehicle may be a word presented vocally. It may be an alerting sign, such as "Hey!" which has no particular signifier except watch out. The relationship between the word and its referent is defined by a rule of contiguity. Event A will be followed by Event B. As mentioned earlier, Werner (1940) described these early mental organizations in which percepts or words are acted on as if they were *things-of-action* as opposed to the later acquisition of words as *things-of-contempla-*

tion. A sign, by contrast, concerns those referent–reference pairs where A is related to B by similarity. Peirce (1958) calls these relationships *iconic.* An arrow has directionality and points; a footprint on Robinson Crusoe's beach on a Friday suggests that there must be another man. The footprint signifies the man who bears the foot. As therapists, we utilize such signs all the time in analyzing the "symbols" of psychoanalysis. Indeed, the psychoanalytic symbol would be a sign using the foregoing nomenclature.

Pars pro toto relationships in metonymy and poorly distributed middle terms in metaphor rest on sign relationships. Jakobson (1956) distinguished between metonymy and metaphor as the basis for contiguity and simile relations. Rosen used this scheme as a means of reinvestigating Freud's Signiorelli-Botticelli incident cited in *The Psychopathology of Everyday Life* (1901/1960). He gave up the primary- secondary-process notion demonstrating the potential in the metonymy–metaphor model for describing the progressive analysis of Freud's slip. This text was also used by Lacan (1956) for reanalysis, using his own linguistic model.

The most advanced form, the symbol, arises only when the referent–reference is arbitrarily related. Humpty-Dumpty's irate protest about Alice's name not signifying her shape is a remarkable example of Carroll's appreciation of symbolic arbitrariness. Except for onomatopoetic words, the relationships of most words to things to which they refer are arbitarary and by convention. As previously mentioned, there is no earthly reason why the symbol *chair* is related to the four-legged sometimes armed apparatus we use to sit on. These distinctions are useful to determine the particular manner in which words are used and responded to at particular times or generally. However, when an individual is capable of symbolic function as a general attribute, he is also capable of perceiving a particular word in all three ways—as signal, sign, or symbol. The American flag is a good example: If we were at war, and the flag appeared on the horizon, it would function as a signal that the ship bearing it was friendly and we would hold our fire. In its format, the flag's stars stand for the number of states and the stripes for the original member states of the union. As such, we have in its sign function a representation of simile of number to its referent. Insofar as the flag also stands for "one nation indivisible, with liberty and justice for all," we have a symbolic relationship of the stars and stripes to an abstract concept.

All three functions ought to be available to individuals who have a healthy capacity to oscillate in their interpretation of words. Indeed, one aspect of the appreciation of humor involves being able to tease out varying levels of reference appropriately. This leaves open the possibility that even a specific word may have a widely held denotation but its connotation and an idiosyncratic personal referent may stimulate a wide variety of potential responses or be used in a manner so as to preclude a therapist's usual understanding.

I would like to emphasize the fact that, although we, in general, talk to patients in words that have rather specific denotations within a language, we are never aware of the congruence of reference until they tell us what are the specific connotations elicited in them. Our general cultural expectations help our understanding, but we certainly have no idea of the idiosyncratic aspects that a patient brings to words from his or her specific environment and past. These are to be uncovered in the course of the exploration of the meaning of the individual's experience as well as his or her manner of encoding that experience in words. The specific examples that follow of this most fascinating function of how words operate and modulate and mediate experience should be instructive:

> A male patient in analysis had experienced prolonged restrictive plaster casting of his legs as a child which required a phase of crawling as part of his rehabilitation to walk. This experience was regarded as a sadistic humiliation at the hands of his physician. When he referred to the analyst a number of times as a "creep" in order to derogate him, he was using a fairly conventional slur. But to him and his therapist the specificity and personal reference was more affect laden than to those who did not know his traumatic history.

> Another analysand met the task of free association with a remarkably coherent story-telling technique. The events of his life were related as a coherent narrative running hither and yon and were always entertaining. Only after a year did he reveal the fact that, as he spoke, he was constantly imaging himself as a trapeze artist swinging on my door. His life history was marked by the need to placate his father by verbal sidestepping and acrobatics, and he carried out similar activities during analysis. That the representation occurred as an image was likely stylistic, but also represented his linguistic activity which was employed in a defensive manner at least once removed from his inner life.

In light of recent emphasis on more immediate experiences in therapy, such as empathic responses, there has been less insistence on the interpretative mode, but even these new approaches do not preclude the considerations noted. Kohut (1977), who relies so heavily on empathy and intuition, advised that these operations are less valuable and reliable with individuals from cultures different than one's own. One would think he believed that empathy is coded as a language and has some of its sources from the surround, just as phonetic memories that are organized as referential systems do. However even if we share a culture, we must still construct a personal history of our patient to bring something uniquely useful rather than culturally general to their awareness.

Just as some would derive discursive and nondiscursive thought and discourse from different functional organizations, others would say that the naming of inner states belongs to a system other than that used for other references. Watson (1919), the early behaviorist, suggested three basic emotions: love, hate, and fear. The similarity of these three areas to Freud's libido, aggression, and anxiety as a core for symptom formation is worth noting. However, though there may be basic emotions, reference demands the dynamic appreciation of affective states under the assigned designator of a code derived from a culture. The socialization of inner states depends on coding them in signifiers that have a carrier potential for understanding among people. We may never know another's thoughts or feelings directly, but we can approximate their significance by use of a common label. Insofar as we know anything about others that can be communicated (or the external world, for that matter), it is in a conventional code. All other knowledge tends to be private.

The gradual splitting off of affective states into discernible units, distinguishable one from the other, is a remarkable achievement of referential systems. One of the tasks of psychotherapy of all sorts is to teach the patient the names of his feelings so that he may apprehend and finally anticipate the life situations or conflicts that seem causative in their emergence. The naming of affects is essential to their taming. Prior tendencies toward action do not permit the stop-wait-think attitudes necessary to exploratory, insight-oriented therapy.

The naming of affects and inner states is variably related to social class and experience. Just as some cultures use a heavy overlay of paralinguistic emphasis and gestural mimetic redundancy, these same cultures tend not to pay much attention to nuance of feeling. When one is poor, one's time is taken to insure survival. The tendency to act, rather than say, as a representation of feeling states is also prevalent in childhood. In this sense, such individuals are responding according to a regressive mode. When Hartmann (1952) discussed the concept of regression, he noted the progressive elements of mental life also had to be considered, insofar as maturation and development created experiences which demanded a change of sign. The wished-for pleasures of childhood so often become the denied avoidance of the adult years. This change of sign is of importance for any dynamic analysis of reference that is useful to therapists.

As noted, reference or signifiers or words may be defined by their features. In the definitional sense, not all words have affective valence, whereas others do. For example, a feature analysis of batchelor includes unmarried and male but would not include good or bad as a feature, except in certain cultural milieus. Indeed, in Philip Roth's novel, Portnoy's mother considered his batchelorhood bad. The chief complaint of some 30-year-old men is their batchelorhood, although sometimes it is rephrased in the jargon of an inability to maintain a relationship. Other words, such as "shit," have affective features to be considered in their definition; for example, slang, unpleasant smelling, etc. The change of sign that Hartmann referred to concerns not only the developmental shift in attitude pertaining to these socially defined lexical items but also to other mental constellations.

To play with one's stool was once pleasurable but was later an anathema. To snuggle up to mother's breast and suckle is the source of an infant's survival and is presumed pleasurable. But later, the same activity achieves a negative valence and change of sign under the incest taboo. Thus, meanings are not static ontogenetically, just as they are variable historically and diachronically. The patient's pregenital storehouse of pleasures that plague him in his adult life were once unadulterated pleasure we suspect. It is the public sharing of such activities with another, even in a small room, that brings them to light in an aura of negative affects—shame and guilt. A curious example of change of sign that has occurred historically in recent years, as well as personally, is the freedom with which patient's discuss sexual activities but not tender or affectionate and sentimental matters so easily.

The latter remark about increased ease at designating sexual events is, of course, only a partial truth. Many people are still reluctant to reveal the intimate details of sexual practice and even find it hard to find the words with which to describe their acts. Moreover, the increasing demands of women for equal rights has given rise to an entire new set of categories to be considered socially and also linguistically. A recent book by Heffner (1978) described the essential degredation of the meaning of mothering. I would extend it to include the idea that even the word is now used in a somewhat sentimental, derogative manner. Heffner suggested that psychoanalysis put a burden on women to mother in such a way as to create better offspring without educating women how to do so; and the women's liberation movement has further torn women from confidence by creating the ambivalence toward mothering that is not easily repaired. Mothering is not only looked at as unessential *but* not necessarily feminine because it is to be shared with males and others. Mothering, then, as a word and concept is an example of how social drift provides a curious wrenching of the features of a definition.

Let me further complicate the matter of reference by introducing the concept of *markedness* and then relating it to a clinical issue that demands attention. When asking about someone's height, we naturally inquire "How tall is he?" Similarly, we say "Is she pretty, slim, lucid . . . ?" To inquire, "Is she short, ugly, fat, stupid?" already implies those attributes. On the other hand, the first sequence of designation is said to include both poles of possibility and even gradations thereof. Thus, "tall" is said to be *marked*, and "short" the *unmarked* of the pair. The implicative reference in the marked word has significance for practice and overlaps to some degree with the labeling of private emotions. An impressive example that has, I believe, gone unnoticed is the word *orgasm*. The literature of the Victorian era and the language of our own period provide some evidence that orgasm is marked for maleness with femaleness implied only secondarily. Although other substitutes, such as *climax* and *spending*, have some potential to refer to masculine and feminine states, orgasm has, by common use, unwittingly and willy-nilly, come to signify what men achieve at the height of sexual activity. Demonstration of this referential markedness comes from three sources: literature, women's liberation usage, and clinical examples.

Pornographic literature, except in rare cases (Anaïs Nin, for one), has been penned by men. Their description of female climax is cast not only in terms of their own experience but is also muddled with that experience. There is a strong tendency to describe in the female an ejaculatorylike secretion at the point of climax similar to that of a man rather than a preparatory lubrication. Peak experiences are formulated for women rather than the actual plateau experiences, which, too, suggests a model based on male experience. Moreover, man's desire for women's desire makes female orgasm seem like a 100% occurrence rather than in reality a sometime occurrence. Parenthetically, this does not imply that males have the same high degree of satisfaction at each encounter either, but a male modeling is still evident.

In this century, the women's liberation movement stems from a background of a fight for equal rights. Women rightfully claim that their labor is as valuable on the marketplace as men's, so why should they be less well reimbursed? Similarly, if sexual activity is a mutual exercise, pleasure should be equally distributed. This also is a warranted aim, but it is possible, as the works of the recent sexologists have shown, that a woman's experience is different—perhaps even more intense—but different, and yet one word, orgasm, is used for both experiences. Separate but equal is very unpopular. Perhaps we are in a polysemantic field: the single word refers to different referents that should be acknowledged by new lexical forms. The word *model*, for example, tends to call to mind *female* as a feature, so convention has led to the cumbersome compound word *male model*. No such convention has yet risen with the word *orgasm*.

Clinically, some men complain of impotence, which usually refers to a complete or partial inadequacy of penile erection. There is also ejaculatory incompetence. Women who complain of orgasmic failure know of what they speak if a simple denotative referent is involved, but the associative path in therapy leads elsewhere. The significance of orgasm becomes enriched to include a sense of relative improverishment and a general sense of inadequacy and need. These associations may be recoded to all that is connotated in the term "penis envy." The experience of orgasm, as designated, is a valid wish. Its determinants, however, may be encased in an associative string leading to a sense of inequality and to relative powerlessness that consciously refers to the desired orgasm but unconsciously refers to having what the male has and of not feeling lesser, deprived, or inept (see Grossman & Stewart, 1976).

This consideration of a difficult area of recent importance suggests how words as references must be engaged at more than a conscious level. Words stand for things and experiences, to be sure, but have dynamic referents and personal referents that must be interpreted in the context of a life, a culture, and a sentence form as well as defined. Indeed, some like Ricoeur (1970) suggest that psychoanalysis is a hermaneutic science. For this latter reason, we must follow our linguistic path yet another step into meaning as derived from speech acts and meaning as derived from interpretation.

Pragmatics and Clinical Work

"But I've gotta use words when I talk to you."

—T. S. Eliot, 1930, p. 152.

Whereof one cannot speak, thereof one must be silent.

—Ludwig Wittgenstein, 1922, p. 189.

The complaining imperative of the epigraph of this chapter appears in T. S. Eliot's "Fragment of Agon." "But I've gotta use words when I talk to you" carries with it an impact that is greater than the sum of its grammatical elements and words. The imperative impact comes not only from parsing the phrase but also from the context in which it is said. These include (at the least) the transactional status of the individual who is speaking, the paralinguistics or pitch tone and prosody of the speaker, and the movements, gestures, and facial expressions that accompany the speech of the speaker. All these behaviors occur naturally and spontaneously and in varying forms and combinations when individuals speak with each other.

The special circumstances of a therapeutic arrangement demands that the text of the complaint be carried out; that is, most psychotherapies depend on the use of words and the request that words be used to convey feelings and ideas. Even images must be translated into verbalizations. The complaint also implies something that has given rise to other therapeutic approaches, such as group touching, Esalen-like marathon meetings, dance therapy, massage, and meditation. Each of these therapies requires expressive interactions or experiences other than talking. In fact, Reich's approach to psychopathology involved not only the development of the orgone box for the transfer of hypothetical energies but also massage for muscular tensions, which were seen as the accompaniments of thought constellations and ideas. Similar attention to the results of ideational complexes has been espoused by Kestenberg (1971), who classified movements in libidinal and ego schemes using dance notation.

The focus on "language as pragmatics" concerns the idea that meaning must be viewed in the dynamic process of communication and not only from contextless grammar. The communicational field may include highly personalized media, such as art or a specific instance of the use of a communal language. Even communal languages, however, take on highly personal significance when cast by an individual tongue. Elizabeth Bates, in her book *Language and Context* (1976), begins her text with the words "Language is a tool" (p. 1). She goes on to say that "We use it to do things," but "unlike all the other instruments that we have evolved to deal with our world, only language can take itself as an object. . . this metasemantic property can lead us into a confusion between the *use* of language and the *content* of language" (p. 1). Our previous discussion dealt with language as a formal system with a syntactic and semantic referential base, whereas this chapter deals more closely with meaning as a communicational intention of an addressor and the vicissitudes encountered as the message is received by an adressee who then must interpret its meaning. The congruence of these elements (message sent, message received) depends on a conventional use of a common social property—words and sentences. A number of other important communicational systems are equally as active at any moment in a transaction, whether that transaction is a conversation or a therapeutic arrangement. Even psychoanalysis, which provides a unique therapeutic arrangement that partially disrupts the usual conversational conventions and rules, can be looked at from the standpoint of how the analyst comes to understand his patient's communicational system and the gradual socialization of communication in the service of mutual understanding via self-reflection.

A number of studies of therapeutic encounters have been carried out as microanalyses of small segments of activity. For example, McQuown, Bateson, Birdwhistell, Brosen, and Hockett (1971) made available the analysis of the natural history of an interview. Scheflen (1964, 1965a,b, 1973) analyzed small segments of the gestural aspects of discourse during therapeutic encounters, and most recently, Labov and

Fanshel (1977) examined the therapeutic discourse of a small segment of a therapeutic session with an anorectic patient by looking at the psychotherapy as conversation. Labov and Fanshel claimed that "at least the therapist should learn to recognize patterns that he follows himself as a speaker and user of the language" (p. 3). They further elaborated that "paralinguistic cues, gestures, and postures may underlie this verbal communication or even reverse its polarity, but they are relatively empty in themselves. All of these investigators have minimized the meaning of what it is being said" (p. 21). They studied the spectragraphic contour of utterances, hesitations, pitch contour, and emphasis and also examined what they call *meta-action,* that is, discussion about what has been said (representations, requests, and challenges) within the therapeutic discussion. Such studies are at the border of linguistics and clinical psychology and are referred to by some researchers as being close to sociolinguistics. Other studies are also available, including libraries of taped psychoanalyses most recently championed by Dahl (1978). However, rather than a discussion of this work in detail, a brief clinical introduction to pragmatics may suffice to suggest some of the avenues that one might want to examine:

> I observed a well-trained young intern taking a history during an interview with an emaciated male patient who had a terminal cancer of the esophagus. Among the routine questions he asked was one concerning recent weight gain or loss. The patient looked at him, searching his face for a response, and said eagerly, "Yes, I have put on some, lately." In discussing the matter afterward, I asked the intern what he thought of the patient's reply with regard to his emaciated appearance and obvious problem in eating. The intern replied that perhaps the patient had been accumulating fluid and that the edema was increasing his weight. He then offered an elaborate, mechanical description, postulating blockages in lymphatic flow, as a plausible explanation for his literal rendering of what the patient had said.

The message offered by the patient was in lexically and syntactically correct speech, and still there was a lack of congruence between the meaning as transmitted and the meaning received. One does not have to be a trained therapist to read between the lines of peoples' messages! However, the example provides us with the possibility that literalness in rendering a message according to a prefixed system may become one of the faults in a communicational process. Certainly, allegorical literature has demanded the opposite of us, requiring that we infer much more than the literal message offers in its sparseness.

The advent of psychoanalysis has permitted individuals to look even deeper, using additional sensitivities to infer and understand

the unconscious messages embedded deeply within simple surface behaviors. The second epigraph, appearing at the opening of this chapter
and attributed to Wittgenstein "Whereof one cannot speak, thereof one
must be silent," might apply here because it is likely that most individuals are silent about that which they have no apparent knowledge. The
impact and meaning of their silence, or their words for that matter, can
only be read through a combination of other signs which the auditor,
trained to listen and observe, can pick out and ultimately interpret. A
lexical-syntactic message may then serve merely as a social wrapping for
a more complex message, whether one is in therapy or conversing casu-
ally.

Both Sigmund and Anna Freud have written thoughtfully about
how the ego is the screen through which the id is seen and that, in the
final analysis, the id is only inferred. There is no mental content which
does not pass through some formalizing structural filter. The expression
in language of some form of postulated id fantasies is that which permits
us to be able to comprehend and interpret their meaning. The meaning
of language in use must be derived and inferred, even reconstructed,
from the data of language *performances* rather than from language
viewed as a human *competence*. The insistence by Chomsky that language is to be studied as competence is the study base of linguistics
involved in an arbitrarily restrictive enterprise. It may now be superseded
by a demanding area of inquiry which is less mathematically precise but
may nevertheless be of major interest to those who do therapy.

The common code that we are using, as we read the text, is not just
a simple, social wrapping, but is accompanied by many paralinguistic
behaviors when a human exchange takes place. As previously mentioned, movement or lack of it, articulatory-vocal intactness or defect,
paralinguistic or prosodic features of tone and pitch, as well as syntactic
style and habitual usage are all important. Thus, language as used by a
person may be viewed as a unique remolding of a social medium of
expression according to the needs and habitual characteristics of that
individual. In short, any utterance will partake of inner and outer demands on the individual, of his personal wishes and social conventions,
and, therefore, is like a symptom that can be analyzed itself.

The other vantage point, the decoding process of the hearer, involves a complex array of techniques for synthesizing meaning that may
include both conscious and unconscious aspects of a message into a
social code which, when appreciated, provides the sense of conscious
understanding. Parenthetically, one should not exclude the possibility

that messages not intended or not consciously understood may be expressed and communicated. Two examples of this have been reported and elaborated in the psychiatric literature. Johnson (1949) insisted on therapy for both parent and child in those cases in which superego lacunae are suspected. Intervention with one party was to no avail, because the parent was conveying one message about his activities to the child, whereas a second-level message of permission to carry out forbidden wishes was conveyed without either party being aware of a second injunction. Similarly, Bateson's concept of double bind involved a primary, socially conventionalized injunction countermanded by a second negating injunction that was usually nonverbal and could be detected in other behaviors (Bateson, Jackson, Haley, & Weakland, 1956; Bateson & Jackson, 1964). The old saw of "Don't listen to what scientists say about their work—watch what they do" would also apply to the problems encountered in studying the pragmatic resultants of language use.

The concept of pragmatics, which Morris (1964) originally described as that portion of language study devoted to the relation between signs and their human users, comes out of a uniquely American school of philosophy called *pragmatism*. Although the school is associated with the name of William James, who wrote a book with that title, the word was actually coined by Charles Sanders Peirce (cf. Gallie, 1952), whose theory of semiotics has been as enriching to linguistics as well as to philosophy (see Chapter 6). As members of a school, pragmatists have been interested in what James called the "cash value of ideas." He went so far as to suggest that the truth value of these ideas could be measured in terms of their practical impact on individuals, and Frege (1949) suggested that there are problems in meaning that cannot be reduced to reference or be measured by their truth value. Meaning is more related to a kind of "Humpty-Dumpty inquiry" that permits words to be used "in whatever way one intends them to be used" to create one or another states of interest or curiosity or excitement in the hearer. It is probably on this basis that the medieval university as well as the nineteenth-century American university placed rhetoric in a central role for study. These universities not only imitated earlier Roman educational emphasis, but, as in the case of the Romans, realized the formative role of politics as the most important activity for human beings. Surely, to be political is to be able to influence with words.

This brief digression suggests that the capacity to influence with words became more important than whether or not the words were true.

The individual capable of influencing another in politics may be *demagogic* or *charismatic*, but when the focus of such influence is diverted to the sick, he may be called *capable of healing*. Each culture adds to the public vision of such individuals by supplying them with certain accoutrements of their trade which then makes them objects from whom we expect special capacities to relieve suffering or to provide a broader vision so that personal pain is diminished or made more tolerable. Psychoanalysts call this the *transference readiness* of the patient which Frosch (1959) described thoroughly in his paper, "Transference Derivatives of the Family Romance." Such specified valuation of the therapist provides a focal point for the rescuing function in the mind of the patient who comes for therapy.

Assuming that most therapists are ready for such patients and wear the cloak of professional credibility, they then have the task in insight-oriented therapies to listen not only with two ears but, in Theodor Reik's term, three ears. Specifically, they are expected to make synthetic use of the data received to bring together that which the patient's own psychological preparedness and state of mind has rent assunder. Indeed, the therapeutic task is to look thoroughly at current behavior (as realistic or as transference behavior) and bring it into relationship with past stored experiences, since our theory suggests that the past has a continuing anachronistic effect on present behavior. To do this, a therapist usually synthesizes an interpretation to which he is compelled by the insistent redundancy of the data presented by the patient. He usually formulates this in a verbal vehicle in talking therapies; if he is a transactional strategic therapist, he might give the patient a task in line with his or her understanding. If he is a classical analyst, he might interpret what he discerns to the patient so that the patient then picks up the cue as a possibility for furthering his or her own inner understanding. There are many times, of course, when the analyst or therapist feels on the verge of understanding the meaning of what the patient is saying only to falter in the exact words. The feeling of discomfort is akin to having something on the tip of one's tongue. Depending on one's style, some therapists share only when they know the entire story with certainty, whereas others share a brief thought and then use the patient's response as a boost for formulation of a more precise statement.

Since we have discussed the background against which pragmatics must be played, it would now be important to look at the varying channels of coaxial communication individually to dissect the pragmatic area into its components. The nongrammatical, nonsematic aspects of the message are referred to as suprasegmental. As previously mentioned, the vocal-auditory channel, the paralinguistic or prosodic channel, and the gestural mimetic channels have been investigated.

First, let us consider the vocal-auditory channel. We find a variety of behaviors that indicates some of our diagnostic prowess has always been derived from the patient's mode of communication. The vocal-auditory channel emits a temporally sequenced set of events which have a short and evanescent period of impact on the listener. We have all learned that the varying stylistic aspects of speech delivery over time signifies a variety of intentions as well as represents psychopathological differences. For example, the slow, plodding delivery of the compulsive speaker causes a degree of irritation in the listener and requires that we hang on every word, thereby revealing the controlling intention of such speakers. On the contrary, the frantic, even frenetic, pace and shrill pitch of the hysteric reveals his degree of excitement, which comes alive in the vocal articulatory channel, and usually accompanies certain tones of seductiveness. Still others may reveal pretension and interest in status by their affected or upper-class accents, whereas others may adopt a speech pattern that replaces "them," "those," and "theirs" with "dem," "dose," and "deirs." Although they are college graduates, such individuals convey personal needs to maintain a nonintellectual facade for a variety of reasons. Adoption of an accent that is contrary to one's background might make one suspicious that the individual might have lived in another country. Such accent might also be diagnostic of iden-tification with the pretensions of the particular area of the mimicked dialects. The choice of particular words of a code, as well as their pro-nunciation, are giveaways for class distinctions, which has been de-scribed in the "U" and "non-U" speech patterns that distinguish the upper and middle classes in Britain from the lower classes. Upper mid-dle class and upper class tend to say *addréss* (with the accent on the last syllable) as opposed to *áddress* (with the accent on the first syllable). Similarly, the word *photograph* marks the aristocrat, whereas *picture* is the preference of the plebian.

During the verbal flow within a therapeutic session, a change in pace or verbal content or a lowering of timbre or pitch are highly sugges-tive of change of theme or a sign that what is being said next may be more important. At the least, the therapeutic listening task involves careful attention to these changes in vocabulary as well as changes in

articulatory completeness or slurring. These changes are common indicators of significance and are included in our observational set though not
often highlighted.

The second focus for suprasegmental interest is the paralinguistic
features of a presentation; that is, those aspects of delivery which lie
along side of the words being said. A major paralinguistic feature is
prosody, which includes tone, pitch, and melody. These features develop prior to the current of messages and serve as the envelope for
words learned at a later time (Stern & Wasserman, 1978). It seems clear
that babies have available the envelope for future speech before they
actually have the lexicon. Moreover, they can make the sounds which
indicate impatience, demandingness, inquiry, being soothed, and sheer
glee, even prior to their being able to express these ideas in words. The
protest in T. S. Eliot's phrase about having to use words is a frequent
one which comes from the depths of regressive wishes of patients who
would rather be held, or experience a feeling of love, rather than sit in
silence and experience the relationship to the therapist in a way other
than having to reveal themselves in words or vocal expression.

It would be the characteristic of a paranoid individual, for example,
to pay somewhat greater attention to the tone with which you said
something rather than to the content of what you said—especially if he
were listening for a specific message of disapproval. In a similar fashion
an obsessive compulsive might pay greater attention to the details of
what you said rather than to the tone of what you said. From the vantage point of a therapist's paralinguistics, a patient once suggested to
me, in a somewhat joking manner, that there must be something more
to be learned from me. Since I, unlike him, was able to offer all my
comments in even-measured, unemotional tones, he knew I had greater
mastery of my emotions than he had. This idea is sometimes represented in caricatures of the vocal and paralinguistic characteristics of
analysts and, indeed, the role may be overplayed by some individuals.
However, insofar as many analysts wish their transactions to have a differential thrust and emphasis, they must exploit the paralinguistic features and prosodic aspects of speech. In the example, given earlier, of
the patient who was putting on weight, one could look not only at his
pleading eyes but also hear the envelope of his comment as conveying
something of a longing for some sign of encouragement from the intern;
some sign of encouragement which would not yield to an explanation of
his increasing edema but would rather indicate that his cancer was not
progressing so rapidly. Lowering one's tone of voice is certainly taken as

a sign of confidentiality, whereas raising one's voice is an indicator of more affective involvement. Controlled measured tones may similarly be a counterpoint against too much affective overload. Anger, when expressed, invariably leads to a rising tone of voice and increasing stridence and pitch.

The gestural mimetic portion of the message is one which has been dealt with most extensively by a separate group of investigators referred to as *kinesiologists*. Although the individual investigators who make up this group do not share a common theory, they all use movement and gestural accompaniments of speech as the object of their inquiry. They tend to be microanalysts of short segments of discussion. Observations far back into the earliest phases of childhood are available. The work of Stern (1971) Emde, Gaensbauer, and Harmon (1976), Condon and Sander (1974), and others direct our attention to the manner in which the earliest human encounters come about and precede linguistic communication. These studies emphasize that the gestural components of contact behaviors seem to be available very early in life and make up an essential feature of the communicational structure between people. Indeed, if language is looked at as only one instrumentality for communication rather than its only instrumentality, one would have to turn toward the gestural mimetic and motor behaviors of early infancy as being prior to linguistic systems. Linguistic systems and codes, when learned, then co-opt the prior gestural and mimetic structures into a harmony of activities, all of which contribute to what Scheflen (1965a,b) and others called the *dance of communicating dyads*. The synergies between observer and speaker are available for all to see in the harmonies of movement between speakers. Being in tune or out of tune, one with the other, may be observed visually as well as auditorily. Facial expressions enliven what an individual says—they lend emphasis and also interest. The difficulties of the deaf are naturally fewer than those of the blind in the degree to which gestural feedback enhances communication. One can only speculate if the higher incidence of autism and schizophrenia in the blind is a partial result of this deficit.

Extensive work has been done on the kinesics of interview exchange between patient and therapist by Freedman and Steingart (1975) and Grand (1977). They suggested that every communicational exchange involved gestural and mimetic features which could be categorized as *representing* and *focusing* behaviors. Representing behaviors may occur, for example, as accompaniments to vocal description of certain items. It is hard to think of describing a vase or spiral staircase without some gestural accompaniment. Contrary to many opinions, these are not regressive motor behaviors reconstituted later in life in difficult circumstances. Gesture is a feature of the representing function itself. Although some cultures accentuate and even encourage such gestural accompaniments to speech, others do not; but gestural accompaniments are not regressive *per se*. On the other hand, the *focusing* aspects of gestures, which may be *self* or *object* directed, may be associated with certain variant behavioral problems. Steingart (1977) showed that, as productive language became more complex, self-directed activities could increase as a means of focusing.

Grand (1977) studied the self-stimulation of schizophrenic and blind individuals as well as those with transitory linguistic handicap. He examined the psychological concept of the self-system as a central regulator of ongoing communication and used the patient's gestures as an "indicator" of such self-regulations. He suggested that hand stroking and self-stimulation could be seen as a way of supplying supportive nutriments for a "coherent self-representation." In circumstances in which such representation could be under threat, as in therapy, or in states of internal discord, an increase of such gestures occurred. Blind subjects, for example, had virtually no object-focused hand movement and other isolated individuals had an increased number of seconds of continuous body-focused movements than those *who seemed* better related. Grand espoused the general notion that touch replaces sight and maintains an inner cognitive model of the self. Moreover, during communicative stress there was an increase of object-focused movements, and this was borne out when an individual spoke a relatively unfamiliar foreign language.

Using a similar model, Grand, Breslow, and Freedman (1979) and Breslow (1978) reported that, when feedback from one's own voice is occluded by an experimental earmuff and an experimental conflict is created, predicted behaviors occurred. Subjects were hearing occluded and were given an interference, such as the Stroop Color Word Test.[1] Self-stimulation increased when voice feedback was reduced and the situation of conflict was created. The experimenters referred to this phenomenon as a *shielding mechanism* that is replete with meaning and posits such behaviors as self-editing when auditory feedback is unavailable.

[1]In this test, subjects are asked to report the color of a series of lines. During the third trial, the interference is established by presenting the words for a color in contrary colored inks; for example, the word *red* is presented in blue ink.

In a fashion similar to the more precise experimental studies mentioned, people have used kinesic interactions as a means of enhancing the understanding of what is said verbally in a transaction. Bates (1976) suggested that "the translation of pragmatic and semantic structures into their cognitive equivalence does not change the fact that these are distinct functional modes during transactions between individuals" (p. 353). This becomes important when one notices that an individual may be saying one thing while doing another and that a dual message is being transmitted simultaneously. Such phenomena are evident during the strict environmental constraints of a psychoanalytic session in which a variety of usual stimuli are interrupted, as by not observing the interlocutor. The patient's body behavior may convey a totally different message than his verbal behavior. Feldman (1959) cataloged a large array of such phenomena in anecdotal form in his encyclopedic *Mannerisms of Speech and Gestures in Everyday Life.* For example, lying on one's hand or crossing one's arms across the chest may convey completely different meanings to the observer than the audition of words. Falling into silence followed by a bodily gesture may be as much an association to that which has gone before as another verbalization. In fact, Needles (1959) described regression to gesture during the course of an analytic hour as being equally available for interpretation in words once a patient is known very well.

Habitual gestures, such as smelling one's fingers or twiddling one's thumbs, may have important significance as message-carrying units. Such gestures become more cogent if they also fit with that which has been said verbally. Caution in confrontation about gestural activities is of consequence; one ought not confront the patient too early, because such a confrontation may constitute an embarrassment unless the meaning of the gesture is preconscious. If the therapist deems it a ripe circumstance for integration of the significance of the gesture with other content, he may attempt to bring it to consciousness. But firmly ensconsed gestural patterns—like tics—tend to be quite ego syntonic, and it would be far more salutary for the patient to be invited to look first.

Jacobs (1973) investigated the gestural activity of the analyst sitting behind the patient in the presribed state of free-floating attention. The analyst may become aware of the fact that he is gesturing, too, or falling into certain body positions which, when understood, may be used as preconscious residues of what the patient wishes to induce. Jacobs suggested that interpretations sometimes become available from these activities just as the dim awareness of an understanding of what patients say emerges out of the continued audition of content of their vocalization.

Having considered all these varying channels of discourse, it is not improbable to suggest that the degree to which primary- and secondary-process modes of discharge contribute to a communicational mode may be represented in a concept borrowed from isotopic chemistry, that is, *relative abundance*. Any particular episode of message transmission may be closer to or more distant from primitive wishes. Since language as a lexical system is ontogenetically, and perhaps historically, in sharp interaction with object relations and affects (which includes such concepts as mother–infant interplay in early infancy), we may be able to construct a system which would involve a hierarchy of communicational stages and use them for better understanding of patients' productions.

Let us reintroduce Werner and Kaplan's (1963) notion that the symbolizing process is a four-way polar sequence of distancing not only between parent and infant but also between reference and object. This distancing may be lessened or distorted at points along the developmental path. On the other hand, there may be extreme instances in which physiognomization and ovall reanimation of thought take place. On the other hand, there may be an overidealization of the word and obsessional isolation of the word from its referent. A variety of dysmaturations and distortions along this continuum may also be described in the communicational process as inferred from gestural and paralinguistic features of the communication. Transactionally, an entire area of meaning may be lost, underemphasized, or overemphasized by alterations in the use of the accompaniments of speech. If one is aware of these aspects of the linguistic impact of what is said, one may be able to systematize observations so that an attempt at reconstruction may be approximated between the use of language and the impact of the meaning of language in use. We may remember Bates's suggestion that language is a tool at this moment and add to it Halliday's (1975) further extension that language is used as a means of getting things done.

To deal with the nonverbal behaviors in relation to their closeness to drives, a taxonomy of behavior may be constructed in relation to the relevant abundance of primary- and secondary-process contribution and how motor-affective and verbal phenomena reflect the degree of primitivity. The following schema is offered to indicate the potential contents on a developmentally ordered sequence which would pertain to the way in which behaviors accrue. For example, gesture and motion are available right from the beginning of life and may be less ordered as idea equivalents than tics—which, unless they are part of the *maladie des tics* and therefore autonomously driven by neural centers, may represent shorthand translations of an ideational content. Hysterical motor conversions, on the other hand, would require a firmly organized ideational content (see Figure 2). The content is out of awareness and then primitively translated into a gestural activity or inhibition. In a similar manner, acting out requires a symbolic translation as in hysteria but is more likely to be the direct translation of a wish into an action without the necessary prior compromise formation.

Affective expression also undergoes a process of developmental differentiation which initially seems to be under the guidance of a general set of feeling states separated, in early infancy, into pleasure and unpleasure. This guiding distinction prevails in later life, and there are individuals who continue to act in accord with this early categorization. For example, neglected and ghetto children tend to act according to a pleasurable-unpleasurable continuum seemingly without concern for whom it is they respond to or without consideration of the social code embodied in the law. As development proceeds, feelings become more discrete and are designated by names. Thus, one moves up a ladder that

	MOTOR	AFFECTIVE	VISUAL	VERBAL
SECONDARY PROCESS	Acting out	Relevance clear and related to context	Eidetic recall	Style syntactic uniqueness
				Word selection
	Hysteria	Feelings unclear in relation to context	Dream	Negation
				Locution
				Incantation
	Tics	Differentiated names of feelings		
		Pleasure-Unpleasure	Imaging (clear)	
PRIMARY PROCESS	Gesture	Tension States (indeterminate)	Imaging (vague)	Primal words

Figure 2. Hypothetic grid of behaviors.

makes the interplay of varying affective organizations and words or names for feelings essential. On a more automatic level, feelings as social communications are articulated in their expression with gestural or mimetic components of speech and prosody. Cognitive awareness of the significance of affects to actions may not be available to consciousness. At the next level of organization, the relevance of one's feelings in relation to ideas becomes clear as feeling states that are without doubt associated with ideational states. The final association with appropriate contexts lends a dimension which permits the affects to be understood and mastered as well as anticipated.

In the visual sphere, certain imaging may be vague initially and may then become clear and registered as a visual memory. Dreams, on the other hand, seem to be translations of highly organized ideational systems which borrow from prior episodic memories that are recast in new combinations requiring linguistic translation. Eidetic recall is common in childhood under sway of mental organizations prior to age 7 (Shapiro & Perry, 1976). However, some persons maintain that facility later in life and, like dreams, translation may be possible.

The verbal sequences in this list of parallel expressions move from primal words in which opposites mean the same through magical and unconscious accompaniments of the use of words as objects or affect substitutes in accord with the scheme first suggested by Freud (1900/ 1953). The incantation takes on value not from its content but from its magical use and ritual function. Like the laying on of hands by a special member of a society, the power of the word, real or created, derives from the mystique surrounding the curing person—or the patient's primitive attribution of power to words. Neologisms are creations of individuals and do not have the advantage of linguistic drift to make them communicative: the more the mobility of cathexis or primary-process activity, the less they will include common morphemes and seem idiosyncratic. Locutions, on the other hand, are the habitual words which are currently in use and not thought to be unusual by patients. They are used as a means of emphasis or of tacitly identifying an individual as a member of a certain group—for example, adolescence.

Negations are placed in this sequence because they have been carefully studied as a specific grammatical and semantic form and have received special attention by therapists, including Freud (1925/1961). He noted that a negation, during the flow of associations in therapy, was an affirmation, that is, it occurred as an association. The negation served as a conscious grammatical device to wipe out the significance of a stated idea. In that sense, negation is a high-level linguistic achievement that may nonetheless reveal the primary-process invoked wish without the patient's acknowledgment. Careful word selection, on the other hand, and syntactic uniqueness as a style indicate the more highly developed characteristic organizations which mark the individual and point to a more organized set of psychic structures.

In terms of therapy, the general approach to pragmatics would then involve the careful observation of all modalities of expression and told experience as a means of making some inference about how individuals bring their ideas together into a coherent system from which the therapist can derive some notion of what we call *ego organization*. Our observational modes must perforce include all communicational channels so that the message that is conveyed is one which is understood in all its nuances and depth. Those investigators who are interested in pragmatics suggest that the semanticists have not gone far enough in suggesting that syntax may be derived ontogenetically from semantics; they would go further and propose "that semantics is derived ontogenetically from pragmatics" (Bates, 1976, p. 354). Even if this is too extravagant a statement, there are some compelling reasons why therapists might be interested in such a vision. On the other hand, such a position does not adequately address itself to the matter raised by Chomsky and Lenneberg about cognitive readiness and parallel developmental structures occurring universally which finally become the tools of communication. Returning to Bates's idea that language is a tool, we must also be able to describe how this tool attains its sharpness and what biological material is used to allow its being so well honed in many, and not at all in others.

8

Speech Acts and Clinical Practice

> *There would not be a call for assistance if there was not a tendency to respond to the cry of distress.*
>
> —George Herbert Mead, 1934, p. 190.

Formal analysis of speech events, from the standpoint of meaning and reference, cannot be incorporated easily into a motivational psychology, unless one postulates an organizational model of mind that includes means–ends sequences or concepts, such as drive reduction involving a release of motor effectors on the efferent side of a hypothetical reflex arc. The latter variety of explanation, used so well by Freud, provided a useful but somewhat mechanistic model of mind. It understands meaning from the standpoint of its biological beginnings and an ontogenetic sequence of overlapping phase- and stage-related fantasies. The derivatives of these basic idea constellations press continuously for discharge in behavior. Such a system links the infant with the child and the verbal adult via the biological substrate but has very little to say about how the formalisms of language intersect with the effectiveness of speech as an action equivalent and modifier in human communication.

One of the critical tenets of behaviorist researchers concerns the notion that the meaning of a verbal act is the response and the contingencies that facilitate responses. The behaviorist eliminates the requirement of mentalist superstructures, because his crucial test is in the efficacy of stimuli in producing responses and learning about the conditions that bring about such responses. I would venture that even the classical psychoanalyst is interested in similar efficacy if he is curious about how interpretation and other verbal communications lead to changes in behavior and symptom dissolution. In a similar manner, the behaviorist would not shy away from the history of a patient's experiences with events, because such memories could be response contingencies that have to be considered. These issues may be formulated in the question of how speaking to somebody effects behavior. They are at the center of such issues as how psychoanalysis, psychotherapy, or any talking therapy work. These questions also have an affinity to pragmatics, because they address language as a tool.

The concept of *speech acts* should have wide appeal for psychotherapists, because it takes a broadened view of speech events, permitting practitioners to include the concept of *intention* with reference and deep structure as determinants of meaning. Unconscious motivational psychology may be partially updated by the linguistic knowledge of the speech-act approach not only because it includes intention as a feature of the meaning of a verbal event, but also because it considers the effect of that implied intention on the individual who hears the utterance or interpretation. Although a generative grammar must consist of syntactic, semantic, and phonological components, the speech act includes such additional elements as a number of social conventions which permit meaning to be read beyond the text itself. Thus, meaning is embedded within the speech act as well as in the context of expression at a specific time in development and social history. Unlike the generative grammarians, speech-act theorists start from experience with language and end up in an abstract and philosophical system. Indeed, their strongest proponent is the philosopher John Searle. However, the application of this system is more promising for those engaged in psychotherapy than is a mathematics of grammar. Perhaps the best way to begin would be to introduce the historical issues that gave rise to the concept of a *speech act*.

The philosophical story goes as far back as Plato. He thought that the idea was more important than the experienced thing—the "shadows in the cave"—that we call *events*. Because events attend to "appearances" rather than the "reality" behind the common sense appearances, they may lead to error. In fact, true knowledge would derive from better understanding of how men organize ideas and how men emerge from the "caves of ignorance" and become aware of the essence of things in ideas, that is, mental processes.

Essentially, this is a rationalist–idealist philosophy, which reached its most expressive stage in Cartesian dualism and later in Kantian idealism. In the Kantian system, "things in themselves" were considered to be unknowable. In the Cartesian system, the secondary qualities impinged on the senses, but the primary qualities of *res extensa* (a thing that has spatial extent) were viewed as unknowable in terms of *res cognitans* (things as known). In the Kantian system, categories of consciousness, which include causal, temporal, and other organizational features of mind, were placed at the forefront as relevant for reference to relationships. Nonetheless, philosophers and epistemologists attempted to make the process of symbolism sensible in relation to this imperfectly knowable empirical world. During the twentieth century, the philosopher Gottlob Frege made the distinction between sense and reference (1949). The easiest example of the difference between sense and reference comes from the discussion by the neo-Kantian thinker Ernst Cassirer (1953).

Cassirer's ideas are worth reviewing in this new context. The Latin equivalent of the word *moon*, *luna*, is quite different from the Greek equivalent *mēnē*. Although both words refer to the same celestial body as seen from earth, the sense of each word carries an impact separable from that which is signified. The word *mēnē* provides the auditor with a sense of periodic measuring and suggests the word stem *mens* —as in *mens*truate and com*mens*urate. Those languages that use the Latin equivalent, *luna*, provide us with the light-giving qualities implied in that stem. The connotations and sense derived from the cognates of *luna* include such mental disturbances as the madness that presumably evolves from an intoxication with the moon, namely, *lunacy*. Thus, the notion is that words express at least two features, one of which is a *thought*, the other its *truth value*. The *thought* that is expressed in a word pertains to its sense; its *truth value* concerns the referent as a class category. We have thus added something new to the triangular relationship described by Ogden and Richards.

A slight digression to a more straightforward linguistic frame of reference is warranted. Cherry (1957) in his explication of the word *meaning* is chary enough to make it a feminine noun and describes it as a "temptress who can seduce the writer or speaker from the path of intellectual chastity" (p. 114). Like Ogden and Richards, he too illustrated the use of the word *meaning* in different sentences to show its varied senses:

1. Saltpeter means KNO_3.   (synonymous)
2. George means mischief.   (intends to cause)
3. He means his father.   (wishes to refer to)
4. Picasso has no meaning for me.   (arouses no emotion)
5. Life has no meaning.   (interest, purpose)

This array of meanings for the word *meaning* is but a single example of polysemanticity and changing sense depending on use.

But to return to our central argument, we note that followers of Frege (1949) among the logical positivist school of philosophy and others became fascinated with what kind of language is permissible in science to reduce ambiguity to a minimum. Bertrand Russell (1949) made the absurd sentence "The present King of France is bald" into an object lesson in reference. What could be the meaning of such a sentence if there is no king of France about whom we can predicate that he lacks hair? Russell used this example as a conundrum to show how grammar and logical completeness may mislead when empirical relevance is sought. Metaphysics can be elaborated into a hypertrophied area of discourse, because words in sentences can mislead and refer only to themselves as they are manipulated within sentences that refer to nothing *but* a mental system. Wittgenstein (1953) looked at language and lexical items to see where language leads us astray and suggested that "languge in use" is the only way in which one could be certain about how to define individual words. He arrived at a very simple distinction, which was already in the air in Kant's writing, that meaningful statements can be understood by virtue of analytic processes as tautologies, that is, equivalence statements, or by empirical and synthetic observations that lead to a concordance between statement and observation. A similar tension is suggested in the Ogden–Richards triangle in which a symbol represents a thought on one side and stands for a referent at another side of the same triangle.

If the discussion thus far seems remote from the problems of psychotherapy, a moment's reflection should reveal that similar concerns pertain to some of the problems encountered with such concepts as psychic reality versus actuality or common-sense reality. It is possible for an individual to build up an elaborate construction that we call a *fantasy* that has sense and, therefore, psychic meaning and that frequently has an impact on behavior. Such a fantasy may be introduced by a patient in a psychotherapeutic situation, although there is very little to point to in the way of an external referent. The therapist's judgment about the continuum, fantasy–reality, will have to be matched to the patient's grasp of what he has constructed versus what he has experienced as though it were real.

Edelheit (1972) advanced the notion that there are primal-scene schemata that dispose individuals to think about human events as triangular relationships among men and women and observers. The actual "bodies" (i.e., specific persons) that are placed in each of these slots have an empirically verifiable set of referents (mother, father, child). But, the readiness for a formal arrangement seems to be a *given:* the specific persons are unique to personal experience. The tautological formal structure is a human universal, and the synthetic variant is able to be indicated or pointed to. Such a proposition suggests a remarkable homology of form to the Ogden–Richards triangle and the interplay of the feature analysis of words within syntactic structures. Whether these formalisms describe the limits of our mind or reality is also a question. Edelheit explored such symmetries in science and language in his paper "On the Biology of Language" (1978). Wittgenstein went so far as to suggest in his *Tractatus Logico Philosophicus* (1951) that we must be silent about that to which we cannot point. The psychotherapist must be content to point to unique mental events as referents that have ideational reality. He then must translate these events into logical and meaningful (and therefore manageable) units and present them to the patient. Only then can the individual in psychotherapy begin to take hold of his mental life, understand it better, find its inner logic or "sense," and thereby direct or redirect his behavior. Beyond this, therapists must also be advised that silence is permitted—it is no shame not to be able to interpret the preverbal. Those who are too certain about that no-man's-land may have to suffer the doubters who will not enter the land of unpointables.

As logical positivism became more and more ensconced within the world of philosophy, it took such extremes as are indicated in Russell's (1949) paper "On Denoting," in which he suggested that words that do not have a clear and certain external referent do not belong in science. This attempt to "clean up" the language of science was met with opposition from a number of quarters. Chisholm (1949) and other philosophers wrote about the need for such terms as "soluble" and "fragile," because they predict or imply regularities of anticipated features of observables. Although the terms are contrary-to-fact conditionals, they help us to predict and provide us with a language for anticipated events as a quality of an object. Imagine a psychiatric nomenclature without such concepts as *vulnerable* or *compensated psychosis* or *mania in remission!*

More important for our discussion of speech acts was Wittgenstein's (1953) ultimate conclusion that language is an instrument and that, in many instances, the meaning of a word is its use in the language. It should be apparent to the reader that the pragmatic position regarding language explicated in the previous chapter has broad authority from philosophy and did not evolve in an intellectual vacuum. While Wittgenstein was working at Cambridge, J. L. Austin, another philosopher at Cambridge, suggested that there are a whole class of propositions that do not concern truth or falsehood but have their reference in the intention to complete acts. The title of his book *How to Do Things with Words* (1962) is most telling. Austin suggested that, when individuals say "I promise" or when they marry and say "I do," these statements are essentially *performatives* which are to be contrasted with *constantives*. Later, Austin reneged on his earlier distinction when he found that constantives turn out to be speech acts and perform as well, so to speak.

Austin enumerated a variety of speech acts (statements, threats, warnings, promises, etc.), and his arguments suggest that there are *extralinguistic conventions*, as Searle (1969) called them, which are as important as syntactic structures, and these extralinguistic conventions are most significant to the transmission of intention and the consummatory aspects of communication. Such a view demands that language be intentional as well as rule governed. Indeed, the term *illocutionary force* was coined by the speech-act philosophers to indicate that every message emanating from a speaker has an intention as well as a grammatical form. Thus, knowledge orthogonal to syntax must be included, because it is important for the understanding of any particular utterance. Moreover, every illocutionary force is designed to have a perlocutionary effect on the auditor; that is, the auditor either receives or does not receive the message as intended and therefore acts or does not act accordingly. The intention to lie is as much a communicational valence as the words spoken, and requires a focus on performance and not on competence issues.

A number of central themes which could be useful to psychotherapists emerge in this brief review. For example, how does the habitual language use of a patient carry illocutionary force? How does the therapist's interventions affect the patient, and what are their perlocutionary effects? How do some patients attend to the literalness of the message versus those elements that provide illocutionary force? How are those elements effected during varied phases of treatment under the sway of the transference?

The speech-act frame of reference requires, as does the psychotherapeutic method, that we listen not only to the words in sentences but also to the intention to be read in each communication. No word goes unheard. The familiar comments that patients make on entering and leaving, before the sessions begin, are as much speech acts with the intent to influence the therapists as any other production. Even when comments are "cut off" and are not a part of the larger corpus, they are directed and said to the therapist. The familiar "Would you mind moving over?" does not constitute a query about the hearer's concern but is, rather, a request to the other person that he vacate the occupied area. Similarly, the patient who requests permission to use your phone or for information about your home life is not just wanting to call someone or curious about you. Rather, the illocutionary force of these speech acts derives from other unconscious as well as conscious intentions. If the unconscious is to be interpreted, it must be attended to and analyzed, not taken merely as a statement to be understood syntactically or as a reference to something going on at the face value in the here and now. It is doubtful that speech-act linguists intended to include unconscious motivation as intention, but, as a therapist, I believe it is a permissible extension that will be forgiven.

In the most general sense, the productions of patients are all directed intentionally toward informing the therapist so that, even when dreams are forgotten or events left out, there is the illocutionary force of the omission to be noted. Indeed, silences must be seen as they are intended, and their significance as a communication has long been witnessed.

The therapist's stance presumes that what is said can be interpreted in the transference as well as in the lexical-syntactic mode presented. The statement "My friend says that psychiatrists are charlatans" may have the illocutionary force of a message to the therapist, although its grammatical form ascribes it to a person other than the patient. Nunberg (1926/1948) writing about psychoanalysis, went so far as to suggest that the intention of the patient is not cure but further regression. This unconscious intention may not be apparent in the direct expressions of patients but in other message-carrying units. "Cure" begins when these unnoticed intentions are brought into consciousness, and the therapist and the patient work consciously toward the same end.

The object of transference—the therapist—becomes the witting target of the patient's feelings and intentions. The speech act permits us to put this force into a linguistic theory only when the formalisms of syntax are superseded, and we reach for a backdrop of motivations or intentions.

Roy Schafer's (1976) *A New Language for Psychoanalysis* may seem to fit the speech-act model because the title includes the notion of a new language. Although Schafer gives no clear indication of having been in contact with Searle or Austin, he was in England during his rephrasing of psychoanalysis, and some of his proposals overlap the speech-act model. He, like Klein and Holt, is interested in doing away with metatheory and developing what psychoanalysts do into a set of propositions that might be restated in everyday language. Even his proposition (Schafer, 1978b) that conflict is paradoxical action and that interpretations must be phrased in terms of the patient as the agent of his actions, which includes his thoughts as well, is a linguistic speech-act notion. This is seen especially in the often-stated analytic locution that the patient wrote the script of his dream; it is not a voice from without. He is set the task of discovering how it came to be that he should write a dream script that is apparently opposite to his conscious intention. He is then asked to take responsibility for that intention by assigning himself a role in that dream. The wishes so discovered may then be assigned to aspects of the self as wisher, punisher, or mediator—in psychoanalytic structural theory, paraphrase *id, superego,* or *ego derivatives*—but all are active aspects of the illocutionary force of the person's productions. No one in such a system may escape his actual and potential active power in his life. No one in such a system is merely a passive recipient of unknown forces, unconscious or otherwise. In such a setting, persons take on responsibility for their lives and their actions toward others.

Considered over longer time spans, the habitual way in which patients present their ideas becomes recognizable to the therapist just as physiognomies become familiar. Varying tendencies, such as the use of clichés, aggressive questioning, and discussing the past rather than the present, begin to reveal other intentions. The speech scripts cover, hide, disguise, and they occur in a regular manner that may be readily understood. Whenever a patient that I had known for many years began his hour by telling me, with self-pitying humility, how inadequate he was, I knew the illocutionary force of his words. They were an intention to hide a conscious sexual fantasy about which he felt ashamed. Whenever another patient seemed to pick a fight and became challenging, I understood that he wished to cover his strong, positive feelings toward me behind which he held thinly veiled homosexual fantasies. Whenever another patient talked of the past, its translation meant that he wished to avoid a current event that he had mixed feelings about discussing with me. Each production disguises while it reveals an intention. The words and sentences are well formed, but the speech act carries its fullest meaning by focusing on intentions, both conscious and unconscious.

From the vantage point of the therapist's productions, we also see intentions. Clarification, confrontation, interpretation, and construction are the traditional tools of analysis. Although their use intends what they describe, their perlocutionary force may miscarry. One of the foremost miscarriages may be seen in the tendency of patients to confuse *description* with a *prescription*. The description of a conflict and inhibition is frequently translated by patients in analysis into permission for action or prescription for action. The injunctions against acting out that are tacit in talking therapies are discarded in the exuberance of a new discovery. Countertransferential investigation must be explored to see if the intention was there in tone, pacing, or timing. Sometimes the zeal for recovery is used by the patient as a flight into health to avoid further uncovering. The therapists may share that zeal in an inner rush to "get on with life."

This last example touches on the action potential of the therapist's words in loosening the patient's restraint. Further discussion follows concerning the efficacy of interpretation, but suffice it to say that speech-act principles provide a powerful linguistic theory to arrive at a model that describes how words carry force that moves bodies. Even though the system is not curious about genetic origins or biological descriptions, it does place human verbal productivity in the arena of action inducers, which may be complementary to the more biological theories of Freud and certainly takes language out of its formal bind. Competence theories may yield universals of language, but they do not describe communicative efficacy of inducing action, performance, or therapeutic change.

Much of the discussion about speech acts has been focused on the philosophical precursors of its emergence and its complementary stance in relation to generative grammar. In many ways, we have come back again to pragmatics and to motivational psychology, which is closer to the interest of therapists. Moreover, the genetic and developmental postulates of psychoanalysis and cognitive psychology gain strength in viewing speech events as performatives and action equivalents. This vantage point has much more to do with persons as agents of action and interaction than with the capacity for nuance of formal structures and the saving of action energy that grammar allows. Earlier interest in thought and language and thought and action receives eloquent possibilities in the speech-act theory.

Therapeutic application may thus be extended to include not only intention, as mentioned, but developmental significance. In therapy, we speak of bringing ego to the fore metaphorically to mediate more sensibly between the id and the superego. We also speak of therapeutic alliance and analysis of transference distortion to help patients toward better adaptation and personality restructuring.

Taking each method separately within a speech-act framework, we may see its use. Therapeutic alliance is a communicational mode which, it is hoped, is dictated by trust and openness. The therapist's words and actions constitute speech acts that permit that to happen. Any insincerity, or intentional malevolence, or self-seeking aim may show through the particular words used. On the other hand, the patient's perlocutionary set provides a readiness to misinterpret the best intended therapist. These distortions usually resonate with and have their origin in past developmental circumstances that provide the network of "wrongminded" templates permitting transference distortion. Therapist and patient alike must have sufficient "observing ego" or objectivity to put those elements where they belong—in the past.

Perlocutionary force that corresponds to a transference distortion represents a psychological set that has to be confronted and undone by words in insight therapies. These words must then be translated into action potentials that are different from habitual organizations. Structural change as a concept then becomes translatable into undoing the tendency to perceive and hear rigidly so as not to misinterpret the present. Such rigid audition must give way to hearing new possibilities and creating new action patterns in life that will feed back and verify the possibility of educating the thought processes to a wider scope of fantasies that are closer to reality. The legacy of having been children and also of experiencing a prelinguistic interval gives rise to distortions of the linguistic period.

In an earlier example, we used the instance of the distorted substitution of *prescription* for *description*. Viewed developmentally, there are potentially rational roots for such an error or perlocutionary rigidity. For example, the toddler, fascinated with his capacity for bipedal locomotion, his recent acquisition of "No" as a tool to retaliate to his environment, and involved in his love affair of the world, as Mahler described it, ventures into the street. His mother pulls him back and, enlightened by reading one of the many volumes on child rearing, explains that he may be run down by a car if he continues his foolhardy activity. We rationalize from our adult stance that she is appealing to his ego and not the anlage for punitive superego functions. It is a description of consequences, not a prohibition prescription on the basis of an arbitrary tug-of-wills. The best laid intentions of mothers and men go astray because that two-year-old child does not grasp causality, is dominated by a feeling of omnipotence, and has an imperfect grasp of words as internal regulators.

An action set is established that may be revived at any moment in an individual's history; that description refers to a mother's words and actions and power politics. That confusion is turned about on the couch or in the consulting room to fit the new situation such that the description now becomes prescription for equally impulsive action in the opposite direction. The perlocutionary force is not that the patient now understands the conflict but that a new version of mother gives permission where once she used to prohibit. The referential distortion of the *who* is also involved in the speech act as well as in the new capacity to understand causal relations. The aggressive element involves interpretation of the act on a permission–prohibition continuum.

As we examine the efficacy of words in treatment, referential features again arise that can be looked at separately from motive and intention. These elements should be scanned in relation to the interpretative process.

Therapeutic Interpretation and Extended Meaning[1]

I have heard of Thee by the hearing of the ear; but now mine eye seeth Thee.

—Job 42:5

Interpretation may be said to lie at the heart of meaning. For example, reference without interpretation carries one to a wasteland of definitions, but interpretation conveys a richness of potential meaning that betrays the human creativity hidden in language. Interpretation during therapy has a similar, special place among many possible verbal interventions (Rosen, 1974). Interpretation of the unconscious, moreover, has become the cornerstone of the classical Freudian intention, and it marks that discipline's unique approach to therapy. If we explore the relationship of the interpretative process in linguistic terms, we should achieve a new understanding that escapes more conventional or traditional approaches.

The interpretation of an "unconscious fantasy" is an event during the course of an analysis which may be viewed as naming. Varying phenomena—motor, verbal, situational, and interpersonal—are synthesized by the analyst into a more or less concise sentence or complex name. This designation can be considered by the patient and the analyst as a common lexical property and can be tested for its congruence with the patient's experience in the past, the present, and the future. Thus,

[1]This chapter is a slightly modified form of a paper, "Interpretation and Naming," which appeared in the *Journal of the American Psychoanalytic Association*, 1970, *18*, 399–421, and is reprinted here with the permission of the publisher.

the patient's words are matched to the things and events of his experience as a first step prior to working through. It is like a verbal note in shorthand, referring to a concept which was formerly expressed only at other levels of behavior. It pinpoints errant experience in a vehicle which can now be manipulated as a shred conceptual property.

Psychoanalysts have long insisted that the analytic situation is a "process" during which the analyst is allied to the analysand's observing ego in an attempt to clarify the "meaning" of the analysand's behavior (Menninger, 1958; Kris, 1956; Loewenstein, 1951). Fenichel (1941) commented that, during this process, "the correct guessing and naming of the unconscious meanings of a neurotic symptom can sometimes cause its disappearance" (p. 43). He further suggested that the next therapeutic innovation in the history of technique was the analysis of resistance. Naming, of and by itself, was not sufficient to cause analytic cure and was later taken up by Loewenstein (1951, 1956), who used a linguistic frame of reference to clarify the importance of verbalization in the analytic process.

Drawing upon Kris's earlier comments about the synthesizing effect of interpretation as an aid to recognition and recall and finally to integration, Loewenstein (1956) commented that "language performs the function of a kind of scaffolding that permits conscious thought to be built inside . . . he [the analyst] lends the words . . . which will meet the patient's thoughts and emotions half-way" (p. 465).

Kris (1950) said that the final integration of the verbal statement changes the patient's attitude from one of "I know" to one of "I believe." In Lewin's (1939) terms, there is a reestablishment of the infantile omniscience. In spite of these studies, Beres (1962) wrote that "the content of the unconscious fantasy, its relation to verbalization and imagery, remains unexplored" (p. 325).

Some years back, Balkanyi (1964), Rosen (1966), and Edelheit (1969) directed our attention to the importance of linguistics to psychoanalysis. Schafer (1976) recently offered a new language with which to carry out this aim, and Edelson (1975) showed the possibility of using generative grammar as a guide to the interpretive process.

With this brief background, one can look at the interpretation of an unconscious fantasy as a verbal event, subject to linguistic formulations that lie outside our particular psychoanalytic science. In my view, the notion of an interpretation as a designative event should enable us to synthesize disparate data which have been collected on the interpretive process. Moreover, the problems which accrue from inexact interpretation or, if I may, from misnaming, can also be understood in these terms (Glover, 1955). In terms of what linguistics deals with as an overall science, we must recognize that the emphasis in this chapter should be on reference as a subsector of linguistic inquiry. However, syntactic and pragmatic concerns are also relevant and were dealt with in another context (see Chapter 5).

Thus far, I have suggested that there are descriptive and dynamic reasons for this approach. There are, in addition, genetic data concerning the early mother–infant interaction in the social process of learning how to name things which could be useful. The naming process is an early feature of object relations as well as a first step in language development (Katan, 1961). Clarification of these events can provide us with useful explanations which underlie behavior seen in the course of certain transference reactions.

Although Freud was originally preoccupied with a neurophysiology of mentation, his earliest thoughts on psychology were well stated in his treatise *On Aphasia* (1891/1953), which antedates his psychoanalytic writings. As previously noted, the very efficacy of the psychoanalytic method rests on a linguistic postulate that thought is trial action and that verbal residues bind small amounts of cathectic energy (Freud, 1900/1953). Freud also wrote extensively on the theme of the relationship of words to things, which is the central problem of the theory of reference. His early topographical theory provided a theory of reference, whereas the structural theory did not. Freud placed the verbal representations and images in the system preconscious. However, he stated, in *An Outline of Psychoanalysis* (1940), that the connections of unconscious residues with memory traces of speech are not a necessary requisite for the preconscious condition.

Beres (1962) later turned his attention to the fate of the verbal content in the situation of descriptive unconsciousness, whereas Hartmann (1952) discussed the fate of the cathexis of these verbal residues. Rosen (1966) suggested that "the conventional shared meaning of words... depend[s]... upon... concepts of referential categories... rather than upon images" (p. 641). He used the Ogden–Richards (1923) formulation to show that the naming process permits reference not only to thing presentations and word presentations but also to concepts (see Figure 3).

As therapists, we should be most interested in how speech influences behavior. Stimulus–response behaviorists and Pavlovian experimentalists have long acknowledged that verbal suggestions can

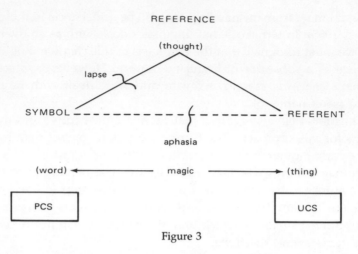

Figure 3

interrupt even reasonably fixed conditioned responses (Watson, 1919; Luria, 1961). These thinkers obviated the traditional mind–body problem by not asking the question "How does the mind influence the body?" Instead they viewed the influence of language in terms of neurophysiological adaptation or simple response systems.

However, many philosophers and psychologists were not satisfied with the black box and the neurophysiological explanations of the organization of behavior (C. I. Lewis, 1949; Werner & Kaplan, 1963). Werner and Kaplan (1963) stated that hypotheses which are based on the idea that words and things elicit similar reactors do not adequately distinguish between reacting and knowing. It is here, in the act of knowing, that naming and mental representation emerge as mediators of behavioral response. "Representation is . . . an emergent activity not reducible to the overlap of responses" (p. 24). This was demonstrated by two conditions: one is the lapse of meaning experiments when a symbol, because of loss of its connection to thing presentations, changes into a mere sign; and the second is the instance of magical speech in which the symbol loses its representational function because of fusion with its referent to become an object in itself (see Figure 3). In the latter instance, for example, we experience awe at the name of God rather than at His manifestations.

The nature of the connections between the things, their labels, and the concepts they refer to can be understood through a study of development. Werner and Kaplan (1963) noted that "objects are given form, structure, and meaning through inner dynamic schematizing activity" (p. 18). We have already alluded to Werner's distinction between things of action in which sensory impressions are bound globally with motor impressions to a later stage of things of contemplation. Only the latter can be manipulated in their own right in the service of representation (Werner, 1940). How efficient it is to have a map to plan a trip "in our thoughts" rather than having to traverse the territory (Sapir, 1921).

During a child's development, his mother's words become an intimate functional complement to his visual, tactile, and sensory experiences of things. That concepts emerge in the course of this growing body of experience is a built-in feature of the human mental apparatus. The tendency of the central nervous system to integrate concepts is paralleled on the level of psychology by the tendency to synthesize and categorize and to make hierarchic organizations in accordance with meaning.

Although the words or phonetic patterns that a child learns may remain unaltered throughout his life, the connotated referent is typically modified by the accidents of experience (Vygotsky, 1934/1962). It is to this area that the analyst turns his attention (Rosen, 1961), because of his concern with idiosyncratic and personal meaning. For this purpose, we must first describe two models for semantic understanding. We have already discussed the referential model and the contextual model in which the meaning of a word is related more to its use in language than to its independent existence as a unit of meaning (Wittgenstein, 1953).

As therapists, we are more interested in ontogenetic changes within the life of an individual than in group usage within a language community over time (diachronic change). Observers of children have described the global use of words as gross referential categories in early childhood that progress to the more specific differentiated uses of words in later life (Stern, 1928; M. M. Lewis, 1936; Leopold, 1939–1949). Transitional forms from a baby word to an adult word are common. For example, the word *boom* has a reference not only to the sound as an onomatopoeic expression, but also to the efficient cause of the sound, namely, to the hammer that makes it. The ultimate reference, *hammer*, may go through a stage of depiction in which it is called a *boom-hammer*. There is a transfer of meaning from the earlier forms to the later forms.

Werner and Kaplan (1963) accounted for this transfer of meaning by suggesting that mental schematizing takes place in a dymamic matrix. Words are apprehended and integrated in age-specific mental structures which remain more or less pliable throughout life. Motor, vocal, auditory, and visual experiences can be transferred and associated one to the other, as for example, in pointing, in speaking, and in reading. In the beginning, words serve as signals or elicitors or inhibitors of action. A later schematization takes place which helps to develop anticipation and symbol function; the latter binds energies in the construction of a representational reality rather than an immediate discharge in response to a specific event at hand.

The further notion that speech is only an instrumentality of language concedes that ideas and thoughts can be expressed in behavioral media other than verbal (Saussure, 1916). It is from this basic principle of organization of thought in terms of meaning that the psychoanalytic principle of rendering the unconscious conscious takes its origins. Thus, to shorten our propositions we can postulate that an interpretation of an unconscious fantasy is the restatement in speech of language expressions formerly indicated by more cumbersome, idiosyncratic vehicles, such as patterned behavior, gestures, and interpersonal and transitional events.

I have already described, under such categories as confrontations, clarifications, and interpretations, a number of possible interventions that occur during the process of psychoanalytic therapy. For this discussion, I shall consider only the interpretation of an unconscious fantasy. To some degree, the technique of psychoanalysis is the required medium in which such understanding unfolds. However, we can use the results of that method to inform other exploratory therapeutic practices and results.

Fenichel (1941) stated that there are three reasons why a patient accepts an interpretation: (1) he recognizes it as true; (2) it is a rationalization in the transference; and (3) it is an identification with the analyst. If it is indeed true that interpretation in its initial phases is naming, what is the referent to which the analyst's words refer? Stone (1961) said it was a "transformation of what the patient has shown into something manifestly different, albeit latent or implicit in what was shown" (p. 26). In short, interpretation is the classification of experience into a verbal message which now exists as an auditory trace carrying the efficacy of speech over action.

The enchanting possibility that interpretation is a synthesis as well as an analysis was brought to light by Mead (1956): "Language does not simply symbolize a situation or object which is already there in advance; it makes possible the existence or appearance of that situation or object, for it is part of the mechanism whereby it . . . is created" (p. 180). It is in this light that classification into names represents only the first step in the analytic process. The "knowing process" not only demands a firm synthetic link between what is said and what is experienced at other levels (in the transference, or in life, or with genetic roots), but also leads to new mental schemata which may be the scaffolding of what has been called *insight*. Thus, interpretation can be a truly creative step.

We now turn our attention to the second step after naming, that is, seeking the congruence between that which is named and that which has been experienced or reacted to in the past. Just as the label *book* which is learned in a specific context is generalized to include the concept of book, the next time an object fitting the criteria is met, so the interpretation must enhance its recall (Kris, 1956; Brown, 1958). Finally, the new name and its variations in experience must be integrated into the system of belief of the individual. Then he may proceed in his future activities with a degree of cognitive control which will permit him to change his behavior in the future.[2]

The process of classification in words begins with the patient's experience with the analyst but influences cognitive structures. Fenichel (1941) wisely commented that interpretations work through one of five avenues: (1) what has been interpreted had formerly been isolated; (2) the patient's attention is drawn to his own activity which he formerly viewed as passive; (3) he comprehends that he had motives of which he did not know; (4) new connections have been made in the associative process; and (5) these new observations correct former distortions. This distinction between simple recognition and insight is no more cogently stated than in the Bible when Job, confronted with God in the whirlwind, states, "I have heard of Thee by the hearing of the ear; but now mine eye seeth Thee."

Since our interest in interpretation must finally focus on insight and behavioral changes, we may use a patient's initial response to an interpretation as a handy observable index to its cognitive and emotional value. To demonstrate that the linguistic view of interpretation had heuristic value, consider the following experiences that every therapist has undoubtedly had with patients:

1. The patient claims not to understand the interpretation, although he can repeat the words of the analyst.

---

[2]Varying explanations of the unconscious meaning of accepting an interpretation have been given. Kris (1956) related the acceptance of an interpretation to receiving the paternal phallus, and Lewin (1950) indicated the oral receptivity of the patient at rest. Interpretation has also been viewed as a gift on the anal level. Although the interpretation of these phenomena seems to broaden the consciousness, they sometimes do not lead to dynamic changes in the ego wherein adaptive behavior and flexibility are enhanced.

2. The patient takes what the analyst says at face value and says that it reminds him of X, Y, or Z, or modifies the interpretation by saying that it is almost so and adds to it.
3. The analyst notices a relief of tension in the patient, though no new analytic work with regard to uncovering and understanding is accomplished.
4. The analyst notices a relief of tension in the patient and has, consequently, a better relationship, such that former negative affects seem to be dissolved, and there is a better working alliance and better object relations.
5. The patient denies the interpretation, either calmly or with increased affect.
6. The patient takes whatever the analyst says and attempts to use it as an explain-all (panchreston).

Consideration of the six phenomena mentioned provides a clinical touchstone to test the use of looking at interpretation as an example of naming.

From its beginnings, the focus of psychoanalytic theorizing has been on intrapsychic processes. In spite of this fact, Freud (1924/1961a, 1924/1961b) found it necessary to consider problems of the ego in relation to outer reality. Moreover, since the method depends on the periodic intrusion of the analyst, he also had to consider the ways of influencing and understanding behavior by verbal exchange (Freud, 1912–1914/1958). The feature of verbal exchange prompted later theorists to reframe the method to account for the communicational aspects of the psychoanalytic arrangement (Sullivan, 1953; Fromm-Reichmann & Halle, 1949). The split between those who continued with classical technique and those who chose other methods is history.

Linguistic models can be applied to the intrapsychic focus of classical psychoanalysis without creating havoc with the method. In Figure 4, the relationship of the potential phenomena can be seen or inferred by therapists and remolded into linguistic terms. The virtue of this system lies in the possibilities of seeing the six patient responses outlined as failures, facilitations, or short circuits in the connections depicted. This model is designed to focus on the area glibly passed over as the "ego function of language." It is hoped that the paths outlined can be helpful by pinpointing where in the language function a defect occurs. As such, one should not be disturbed at not seeing the usual psychoanalytic references to defense or resistance. These references are understood as

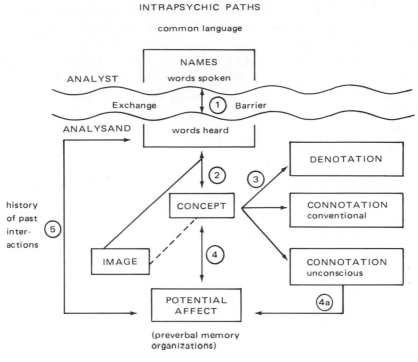

Figure 4

given and enter into the reasons why changes occur in the language function. This is a schematic statement of where they occur and how many dynamic operations share a final common pathway of expression through defects in language.

The words spoken by the analyst are understood by the patient because they share a common social code and they speak the same language. There are many slips between words as intended and meaning as understood, of course, and this is accounted for by what I have labeled the *exchange barrier*. It is to this area that linguists concerned with communication have devoted their energies and the speech act and the pragmatics schools have their focus.

The words or names must now be associated with other aspects of the cognitive-conative system for "knowing" (as opposed to reacting) to occur. The words are associated with concepts that correspond to the denotative meaning of a word. This feature has the immediacy of gestural pointing. The relation between denotation and connotation may be two-pronged; changing usage provides a history of meanings which are cluttered about a word, and these remain available for social purview. It is also permissible to extend connotation to include the history of its use by an individual. In this sense, connotation may include genetic linkages which are unconsciously significant. In all these instances of concept, denotation, and connotation, there may be associational linkages which are horizontal at a single level—from word, to word, to word; or vertical—from denotation to social historical connotation, to personal ontogenetic connotation.

In unconscious connotational systems, there are connections to affective residues which may be loosely organized in the same schema, but not necessarily as verbal residues (potential affect) (Freud, 1900/1953; Schachtel, 1959). These latter linkages enable the preverbal schema to be related ultimately through the associational chain to verbal-discharge as well as visceral-discharge channels, as is presumed in psychosomatic illnesses.

This scheme is couched in linguistic terms but includes the same postulated and observed connections which psychoanalysts have used for some time in their clinical understanding. The six paradigms can now be considered in relation to the paths described, and, in addition, each paradigm will also be viewed as an arrest in the development of reference and be made more specific with clinical examples.[3]

1. The situation in which the patient can repeat the analysts's words without knowing what they mean is akin to lapse of meaning experiments (break between word and concept). During these experiments, subjects are asked to repeat a word until they finally experience a loss or diminution of its rich meaning while still feeling it is a familiar word. The connotations with the concept and thing representations to which the words refer are lost (Jakobovits & Lambert, 1961). It is like a reversal of aphasia wherein the words are available but are not linked with cognitive schemata except for the automatisms of syntax.

During the analytic process, this phenomenon occurs in certain patients who encode into words with diminished reference to concept or consideration for communicative value. They string words together for a kind of *Funktionslust*, which is akin to the stage of babbling in early

---

[3]By analogizing the breaks or slurs in connections to developmental stages, no equivalence is implied. Hartmann (1952) has suggested that, in regression, patients do not act as two- or three-year-olds do. There is an alteration in function in the fact of structuralization which is established. Thus, functional alterations occur along the "faults" in the developmental lines.

infancy or of learning rhymes and catechisms by rote at a later stage. There is a hypercathexis of the lyrical poetic function of language (Jakobson & Halle, 1956). The hearing but not the understanding is often accompanied by keen sensitivity to how one says something rather than what is said. The potential for paranoid misunderstanding is evident in this type of language arrest.

A similar defect in knowing may serve a defensive purpose in the well-known pseudonaiveté of hysterics. The functional link between what is designated and what is known may be lost in the service of a wish to keep out of awareness a potentially painful affect associated with remembering. One sees this dissociation of name and concept in the defensive isolation of obsessional neurotics as well. This link between hysteria and obsessional states, because of their descriptive similarity, is more likely due to factors of ego organization than factors ascribed to libidinal organization. The different levels of libidinal fixation observed in each of these neurotic types are expressed through a final common pathway describable in the terminology of linguistic reference.

2. The instance in which the naming of an unconscious complex leads to slight verbal modifications by the patient or increased flow of associative themes is the opposite of what we seen in responses of Type 1 (there is facilitation of links of word to concept and deep connotation). In this type, the name, the thing, and the concept referred to are well coordinated, and congruence is immediate, which corresponds to Kris's idea (1950, 1956) that recognition stimulates recall and finally integration. For these reasons, the interpretation is said to be well timed and already preconscious. The analyst's proposition "fits" what the patient feels; that is, its connections with experience and, therefore, its integration into a complex, personal-meaning schema are secured by the observer giving it a name. This concept of "fit" must be related to "meanings" which are personalized syntheses generally not available to veridical demonstration. The "aha!" or "light-bulb" phenomenon is more akin to a truth function with is nonexperimental, nonrepetitive, and highly egocentric. Its validation rests on continuing the match of experience to proposition.

The particular terms in which therapists couch their interpretations are geared to estimates of "receptivity" of the patient. We know, for instance, that many therapists use anecdotal styles and others offer direct statements. With children, we use concrete terms with strong referential links to current play material. Glover (1955) advised interpreting only in the transference as an attempt to appeal to the patient's immediate designative experience as opposed to something more remote.

In interpretation, what is sought is naming at a level which the patient can use (Hartmann, 1951), and linguists provide many examples of this process seen in childhood. Those who have attended to the interplay between mother and child as language is taught attest to the gradual development of lexical forms. Not only does the mother speak baby talk at first, but the parents echo the child as both parties seek congruence (M. M. Lewis, 1936; Brown & Bellugi, 1964). The flexibility of the parent in permitting transitional forms permits a growing sense of autonomy for the child.

This evolution of designation to more standardized socially shared forms is akin to interpreting from the outer, more manifest derivative experiences to the more concrete or archaic representations of these experiences. During psychoanalysis, the process is often reversed, going from the concept to the particular, the recent to the past. This process not only attests to the particular state of the synthetic function of the ego (will the patient understand) but also to the actual stages of learning to name as a means of coping more efficiently with the world.

The following example of broadened insight during analysis was derived from the discovery of the meaning of a childhood name which a patient used to designate his mother. It provides a concrete example of the meaning of "analyzing from outward-in" as well as an indication of the spreading effect of understanding:

> The patient, in his mid-twenties, had succeeded in extricating himself from a marriage in which he had a strong aversion to sexual contact with his wife which was associated with impotence. He complained that his wife "clutched at him" and that he felt hovered over and restrained with her.
>
> His mother had been and still was a strong influence in his life. He never felt any achievement was his own, but that his mother intrusively shared everything. This feeling was so strong that at times he preferred failure to success rather than share his success with her.
>
> Much of his feelings had been interpreted in terms of the concepts outlined. Only later did he reveal a childish name he had for his mother which had two variants, "poomie" and "pooshe." The first stood for "poor mother," the second, "poor she." At the time the words were coined, his mother had often been sick. During the discussion of his mother's sickness, he mentioned his own suffering and deprivation during the same period. I interpreted the necessity of two names to mean that one of the poor suffering parties was himself; consequently, not only pooshe (*poor she*) but also poome (*poor me*). This interpretation led immediately to his expanding on his own self-pity not only in the past but also in the analysis. Furthermore, he remembered that he had not called his mother "mother" until after she had forbade his using the

other name, which she deemed babyish. He felt very strange calling her by a name which other children used to call their mothers. Also he wondered if she would know it was "her little boy," since the name was not personal.

The interpretation of this case revealed the symbiotic closeness which the childish names denoted. Then, at a later date, the patient was able to consider the Oedipal manifestations of this early feeling in the form of a wish that his mother share his penis, which was reinforced by her constant intrusions into his privacy and successes. The latter may be considered an archaic concretization of the more general concept presented earlier in the analysis and belonging to a different developmental epoch.

Associational links will often lead to expanding of consciousness but not necessarily to new adaptations, because the affective aspects of the transference are also integrals in the knowing process. Thus, although a facilitation may be evidenced at the junctures 2 and 3 (see Figure 4) between words, concepts, and connotations, this does not guarantee that the link to affect is secure.

3. Interpretation at times yields a relief of tension without any new uncovering taking place. It is a situation that evolves in patients who have specific ego structures with relevant genetic histories. In such patients, there is a short-lived facilitation between words and feelings, but there is no evidence of connections to associated connotations at the same or at a deeper level. These are patients who beg the analyst for more activity during the course of analysis. If this wish elicits stubborn refusal on the part of the analyst, it only produces more tension. On the other hand, if the analyst complies with the request, there is no furtherance of the analytic process because the patient is constantly gratified. As Freud commented, we travel indeed between Scylla and Charybdis!

Another case of an immature analysand provided an example of this type of nagging attitude which was not only the replay of an unconscious wish but was also a conscious repeated experience within his family. He was truly and descriptively an obsessive nagger.

The meaning of nagging behavior is surely overdetermined but is also related to a fact of language learning. As an example, one day, in a playground, I noticed a child of about 14 months who had obviously just learned a minimal vocabulary. She was sitting in a swing while her mother continued a casual conversation with a neighbor. When an airplane passed above, the child looked up, pointed to the sky, and made a roaring sound, which was her onomatopoeic designation for the plane. She looked at her mother and again made the roaring sound, but her mother paid no heed. The child again made the roaring sound and looked at her mother. She persisted in this vocalization until the mother acknowledged her sounds and turned to her saying, "Yes, dear, that is an airplane."

This anecdote points to the dynamic matrix of mother–infant interaction in learning language. M. M. Lewis (1936) showed that mother and child gradually come to a congruence at a middle ground closer and closer to lexical speech. In a later study, Brown and Bellugi (1964) showed that even though children at an early level speak telegraphic syntax, their parents always answer them in an expanded syntactic form and that the interchange goes on until it is finalized by the parents' reiteration. Thus, the child comes to expect that, to end an exchange, the mother must naturally repeat what has been said. In this sense, the development of naming is keenly attached to the relaxation of tension through affirmation by repetition. I would suggest that, in patients of the type I have been describing, the tension-relieving aspects of the analyst's talking is what is being sought and that the words are less relevant. It is a characteristic of these patients, however, that the relief of tension is short-lived and the nagging begins again.

4. There are situations in which interpretation yields a marked tension relief with dissolution of former negative affects. Better object relations and a working alliance ensue. This situation usually leads to favorable analytic work. As we have seen in the response to the third paradigm, there is a facilitation of the path to affect with gradual opening of paths to concept, finally leading to connotative associations. The cognitive links develop only later through the new work made possible by the feeling of alliance to the analyst. This situation also attests to the close connection between the naming process and the human matrix in which names are learned. However, in this instance the economics of tension relief without conscious understanding has priority over the cognitive steps.

We see a similar sense of relief when remembering words that are on the tip of the tongue; that is, the linking between a verbal vehicle and a preconscious referent. When the therapist interprets an unconscious dynamism correctly, the "naming of the enemy" elicits a new sense of ability to cope. Most likely the catastrophic reactions of aphasics are partly due to the frustration in their inability to master the efficiency of thought by naming or, better still, through "verbal thought." This developmental link between object relations and thought organization was recognized by Abraham (1924/1953), when he constructed a table of vicissitudes of the development of libido, which he coordinated with preambivalent, ambivalent, and postambivalent attitudes toward the object. Although many ego functions mature free of conflict (Hartmann, 1939/1958) often this development is intimately tied to fantasy organization (Peller, 1964). A derivative behavior has connections not only with referents but also with organized schemata tied to affects. Sometimes affects are freed before the referents can be used for "knowing."

As Freud pointed out, a cigar is not always a phallus; similarly in child analysis, a truck is not always a penis. To interpret correctly one must wait to see the particular meaning at the particular time in relation to the level of the transference and context. Although at each moment in time the individual is expressing all the multiple functions to which Waelder (1936) alluded, the level of fantasy organization which is most relevant at the time is the one which has to be named. The sense of relief the patient gets when the immediate concern is accurately designated calls into effect the second step in knowing—seeking of congruence— which leads to secondary correlations with more remote experiences (see paths 3 and 4a in Figure 4). On the level of object relations, it is akin to saying to the parent "You have given me the words to designate my experience and it works for me, and, therefore, I feel more trust toward you and can also fit other experiences to the words."

5. Often interpretations are met only by denials or denials with an increase in negative affect. We are acquainted well enought with Freud's paper on negation (1925/1961) to present negation in the contexts in which it is placed by symbolic logicians; specifically, to represent a negation one must present that which is being negated. Negation does not stand alone but represents a judgment about a proposition. Thus, in the course of an association, a denial represents an affirmation. We sometimes use a negation as a means of demonstrating the validity of an interpretation. This has always seemed a rather spurious kind of verification, leading critics of analysis to suggest that the patient is in a coercive bind. Yet, we know that analytic data often follow negations which verify what has been denied. Thus, the facilitation at path 3 (Figure 4) is what analysts use as verification, without too much protest.

For example, during the analysis of the patient described previously on p. 112, he presented a dream and raced through his associations, obviously shifting to a content which bore little discoverable relationship to the manifest content of the dream. When he was asked for further associations to the dream, he balked. I interpreted his resistance as a parallel to his feelings in marriage that the longer he stayed with his wife, the more he felt trapped by what others expected of him. He denied this with little affect and proceeded on another track. Later, he slapped his head and noted that he had said "No," as he had so frequently done with his wife and mother, because he could only feel free and autonomous when he opposed others. He felt that what they or the analyst said were challenges and were therefore to be denied. Another variant he often showed was "All right I'll do it your way." Although he complied on the surface, he maintained a stubborn resistance to getting anything out of his compliance because for him it was nothing but an obedience to another person because of guilt.

Developmentally, the use of negation represents another link to the interplay between two parties seeking congruence between the symbol and its referent. Even though negativistic two-year-olds say "No," they show comprehension by their very opposition. It is not of passing interest that negative forms are learned late and with difficulty by young psychotic children (Shapiro & Kapit, 1978). In the analysis, negation is a frank continuation of the ongoing dialogue; what has been named has been heard, has been integrated, and can be used for further exploration if the opposition is lifted; that is, if the word has been sufficiently related to its concept. What is lacking here, if indeed the negation does turn out to be an affirmation, is the part of the sequence which guarantees insight—congruence seeking and belief.

Once classification is secure, congruence and belief depend on the recovery and elaboration of other experiences past and future (a facilitation of paths 3, 4, and 4a in Figure 4). In effect, Glover's admonition to interpret in the transference prevents evasion by negation because only those things which can be pointed to with the finger are interpreted.

6. The notion of an "explain-all" was brought to our attention by Szasz (1957). Naming may give the patient a dynamic feeling of having discovered something, but this sense of discovery may further inhibit his activity. In the course of the therapeutic process, one sees this in the patient who uses the interpretation of an obsessional manner and applies it in an across-the-board manner to everything he does (a facilitation of paths 1a and 2 in Figure 4 with an overuse of path 1). Often, at a later date, he finds a situation in which the interpretation does not fit and is furious with the analyst, saying that the whole process is useless. This situation is often due to an initial idealization of the analyst and a later wish to destroy his authority.

In another example, a patient in his late twenties was having sexual difficulties with his wife because of the encroachment of a typical madonna–prostitute split. The interpretation was offered that, since he married his wife, he was unable to seek genital aims with her because she was the one who, like his mother, cared for and fed him. There was ample evidence for this interpretation, and it led to further insight and understanding. Later in the analysis, whenever a new sexual problem arose, he would bring out the "old saw" to explain his reluctance, although new data were prominently available. At varying times, the new data clearly related his wife to his sister or involved his fear of the vagina or his shame regarding pregenital aims to a homosexual object choice. He would stubbornly deny these new interpretations reverting to the original interpretation. This was the "name of the animal" so how could it have another name.

In his early development, a child may use the word *dog* to describe all four-legged animals as though dog were the generic class-inclusive term. An arrest at this crucial stage may ensue if his learning is contaminated by the sadistic struggle over toileting. At a later stage, the parent may help to ensconce such attitudes by saying to the child "God made it." By decreasing his curiosity with a name, the child proceeds as though he had an explanation. Linguistically, the latter represents an overvaluation of the word and name as information as opposed to the word classification. It may be akin to the fusion of concept and word as seen in magical speech—the mere pronouncement causes change. The spuriousness of this claim is gained through later experience.

In summary, the interpretation of an unconscious fantasy is a necessary first step prior to working through. The therapist provides a shorthand verbal representation of what the patient has formally expressed in nonverbal behavior. The verbalization is viewed in the light of linguistic models of naming. The theory of reference, formerly available in Freud's topographic theory, is lacking in the structural theory. The linguistic models presented here are designed to describe the vicissitudes of verbal representation according to what is known about the development of reference. In this way, disparate data on the interpretative process are brought together under a single heading known as *the ego function of language.*

10

Identification, Identity, and Language Structures

Its [identity's] most obvious concomitants are a feeling of being at home in one's body, a sense of "knowing where one is going," and an inner assuredness of anticipated recognition from those who count.

—Erik H. Erikson, 1968, p. 165.

Piaget (1970) described a structure as a "system of transforms." Although this may seem an adequate definition from the standpoint of modern structuralism, and for the purposes to which Piaget used his definition, it is not one to which all structuralists would agree. It is a difficult task to put together into a single group certain philosophers, the French anthropologist Claude Lévi-Strauss, and the psychoanalyst Jacques Lacan. Indeed, the tendency toward vigorous individualism of thought among the group of thinkers so classified is such as to defy any simple category or designation. On the other hand, there seems to be a general approach which can be said to characterize all "structuralists" which has significant application to psychotherapy and our understanding of personality.

Studied from a historical vantage point, structuralism derives from the study of language itself, only to attain a broader focus in philosophy and anthropology at a later point. If Saussure is described as the "father of modern linguistics," he is so designated because he demonstrated that language may be studied as a synchronic system whose organizational or structural features may yield significant insights. Language study up to the point of Saussure's creative efforts had been largely diachronic; that is, it was the history of language forms, drift and etymology of words, and their relationships to meaning. With Saussure's research, there was a shift in interest to the relationship between the sign and its meaning and ordering in sentences; these organizations or structures were to be studied independent of speakers performing particular speech acts. Interestingly enough, during that same period of the twentieth century, philosophers began to reexamine their historic roots in the light of the exuberance of the new physics that seemed to explain so much. They tried to rid philosophy of metaphysics and sought a unity of sciences based on the model of physics and leaned heavily on the analysis of the language of philosophy. However, there was a reciprocal trade-off with the new linguistics in that, as philosophers became interested in the meaning of propositions, some linguists took on an atomistic approach attempting to join the unity of science movement. As mentioned previously, Bloomfield (1933) built his system on a set of hierarchic structural organizations, with each higher level successively explainable by that which was at a more elementary level. The structural organization of language was viewed homologously as atoms building up to more molar entities and then interacting in fields. The properties of the lower-order phones and phonemes provided for morphemes and words and finally sentences. Bloomfield sought an empirically sound linguistics based on successive structures rather than on a wholism which was understood by transformational analysts. It was a model that was closer to physics, although it prescribed structures they were not structures in the sense of modern structuralism. Indeed, the efforts of linguists like Bloomfield was an attempt to "scientificize" linguistics.

Philosophical statements were analyzed linguistically by such new schools as the Vienna Circle and the Logical Positivists, and meaning was sought in empirical confirmation and congruence between that which was stated and that which could be observed. All else was reduced to tautology or nonsense. On the other hand, the newly developing philosophical systems, which were critical of the stringency of the positivistic models, suggested that man's scientific enterprises in areas of investigation other than physics required other validation than repeatable empirical observation. New approaches suggested that "truth" could also be served by a rule of coherence. Conceptual fit and explanatory power on the basis of fit could also lead to new insights.

It was David Hume who, in the Lockean tradition, looked at all that is in the mind as having been first in the senses, and who described the potential fallacy of causal analysis. He proved that contiguity of events

may sometimes lead us astray and provide us with the erroneous conclusion that, because event A precedes events regularly, A causes B.
This propositional analysis provided the sexagenarian Immanuel Kant
with the impetus to write his major works; he even credits Hume with
waking him out of his dogmatic slumber. Causality and other categories
of consciousness, as Kant described them, may be structures of the
mental apparatus itself and not simply "out there" in the world from
which percepts emerge. The Idealist school of philosophy, including the
modern thinkers Cassirer (1953) and Langer (1967), advanced the view
that one might better study the structure and organization of mind to
understand how order is placed on the phenomena in nature rather than
study nature as a simple source of stimulation. If these organizational
structures and their natural inputs are related in a one-to-one manner,
then the materialist–mentalist confict might no longer be a problem.
However, whether this is so or not, the Idealist alternative clearly fo-
cuses on man again and his structuring capacity, which is exemplified
best in his linguistic potential to describe nature.

Piaget demonstrated that mathematical structures are so simply observed and immediately apprehended because of the operation of reversibility and conservation. Given the rules of numerical systems, one plus
one always equals two. Similarly, two minus one always equals one. If
one of the basic elements or rules of that structural relationship were
altered, the entire formal unity falters, and a new method of analysis
must be constructed. Similarly, given the assumptions of Euclidian
geometry, the interior angles of a triangle always add up to 180°, but, if
one of the basic structural rules were to be changed, a different variety of
geometrical system would emerge which then would have to be analyzed
for its internal coherence and its variant products.

What does structure have to do with psychological systems and
especially psychological systems that have clinical application? Are we
once again in the predicament of lumping together dissimilar disciplines
under a common abstract rubric? Will the application of such an analysis
bear practical fruit? Suffice it to say the matter has been introduced with
an intention to explore its significance. Moreover, therapists and personality theorists have become linguistically prone to speak of personality and character "structure": we use Freud's "structural" theory; Kernberg (1977b) writes of "structural diagnosis"; and therapeutic gains
are looked at in terms of "structural" as well as practical changes. Unless
these psychological investigators are using the term *structure* anomal-
ously, we ought to be able to examine what is said of structure in a
general sense to see if it applies to *clinical constructs*.

Piaget (1970) designated three key ideas essential to structuralism: (1) wholeness, (2) transformation, and (3) self-regulation. By *wholeness* Piaget meant the tendency of structures to be perceived as wholes and not additive of smaller units. The easiest example of this view is seen in gestalt psychology, which prescribes that perception of form takes place within a context of wholes rather than being made up of the sum of its parts. For example, an arrangement of crosses in a circular form is perceived as a circle, and its property cannot be accounted for on the grounds that it is made up of X number of crosses. Transformation provides the possibility of novelty emerging from a small number of basic units. What is structured and subject to analysis are the resultant molar organizations that can then be viewed as resulting from transforms of the basic elements. Kant's categories of consciousness are similar, and, as we explore further Chomsky's notion of transformations in grammar form from a base deep structure to a surface structure, we find a system that also qualifies for inclusion as a structuralist model.

The notion of self-regulation involves the possibility of feedback and cybernetic loop such that the individual applying the transforms either consciously or unconsciously is always able to be in homeostatic balance not only with nature but also within himself, intrapsychically. It accounts for such features as rhythm, regulation, and operation in a biopsychological field and further permits that structures may emerge in time which are not reversible but creative of new hierarchic arrangements. These, in turn, can account for new behaviors or features of a system not available at an earlier level. The latter would be contrary to one of the early rules of mathematical structuralism but is introduced to account for biological systems. F. H. Allport argues cogently in his book, *Theories of Perception and the Concept of Structures*, that we would like to avoid a rigid architectonic vision of structure rather than one which allows dynamic interplay within and between systems. These models recall Hughlings Jackson's view of brain damage which leads to behaviors that might be looked at as a dissolution of function with a return to lower organizational principles. Although this model was introduced in the nineteenth century, it seems to be rather modern. Indeed, Freud himself, quite taken with the potential of Jackson's formulation, adopted many of its features in his own model of mind, again attesting to the significant role that language-function studies played in theory formation.

The three variables described by Piaget can then be used as guideposts to examine psychological structures. These same psychological structures can then direct our attention to clinical issues in order to see how language, as a structural organization, may be used as an observable parameter than can help us to define an aspect of what is meant by ego organization in specific personalities.

Rosen (1961) used an epigram, attributed to Molière, which states *"le style, c'est l'homme même"* (style is the man himself). How can we construe such a statement when psychological organization has been viewed for so long as a synthesis of fractionated ego functions, a variety of impulses, moral controls, and homeostatic regulatory principles that govern all? It suggests that whatever goes into style or our perception of style, as a whole, is not reducible to individual parts that make it up as additive of those parts. Stated in this manner, the proposition takes on a structuralist cast. Moreover, we are provided with a general proposition which also has developmental significance and permits the psychological roots of character formation and identity formation to be reorganized continuously during the course of development into new and more complex structures. One of the earliest formulations in this vein comes from Wilhelm Reich.

Reich (1928/1948, 1929) looked at character as emerging from the layering of structural organizations, each of which is the outcome of a resolution, at each successive developmental stage, of the struggle between libidinal and ego forces and the adaptational requirements of reality. He used the metaphor of "layers of character armor" which then could be peeled away or "attacked" in therapy, reestablishing as conflictual that which no longer appeared as conflict but as character structure or, using our later notion, *style.* In working through the defenses encountered at each level of organization, the analysand appreciated the neurotic core which was the historical basis of the particular character structure that presented at clinic. The task in therapy was to deal with the character armor at each level, to undercut the ego syntonic support, to reveal the wishes and impulses which sustained the need for each structure, and then to undo the structure to provide a new path for the possibility of "healthier" and more adaptive character formation.

Although most psychiatrists, even those within the classical school, do not adhere to the somewhat militaristic view of character armor and struggle at each level, the Eriksonian epigenesis and consequent descriptions of character emergence in interplay with varying cultural demands are not dissimilar in form from Reich's model. Nor are the Reichian models dissimilar from Freud's early characterology, which was based on varying libidinal stage wishes and defensive organizations that were reflected in varying character traits of the adult personality. Indeed, even if one does not accept libido flow as a quasi-organic maturation, it has been clinically demonstrated that certain character constellations, such as parsimony, cleanliness, and orderliness, do appear together in character organizations. Even if one were no longer inclined to call these individuals "anal characters," the genetic nomenclature points to character as emergent and developmental with structuring precursors rather than creations *ex nihilo*. Indeed, much of what the modern depth analysts have described in the way of severe character pathology, including narcissistic disorders, borderline conditions, and the like, are capable of analysis as disorders of transformation and their consequent imperfections of wholeness. If approached in this manner, any character structure would be envisioned in terms of its current organizational features as well as its analyzable potential relationship to early developmental landmarks.

The propensity of individuals with severe character disorders to use certain defensive operations (rather than others) which are disorganizing or reality distonic to save their organizational sense of wholeness is well in line with a structuralist point of view. Maintenance and regulation of self-esteem are central to our concept of severe character pathology. These may be construed as structures that tend to persist and are generally difficult to reverse. Piaget's discussion of biological organizations applies here and allows emergent structures over a period of time in a developmental path to have a final form resistant to change. In this sense, biopsychological emergent structures differ from mathematical or physiochemical structures. However, therapeutic interventions aim at disrupting these emergent, more-or-less fixed structures to redirect the personality toward new adaptations. In this sense, even biological structures would obey the rule of reversibility, if we had the key to unlock structures.

In a biological organism such as man, certain self-regulatory functions have been identified as operating from the beginning of life. Authors have looked for their expression in such concepts as congenital activity type (Fries & Woolf, 1953) or temperament (Thomas, Chess, Birch, Hertzig, & Korn, 1963). The identification of tendencies toward rhythmicity and approach behavior permits the environment to match or miscue the biorhythms. The child, growing up, responding, and chronically adapting, may develop a variety of fixed inner organizations that permit or reject the likelihood that talking will be influential toward change. In this sense, psychotherapy may become an unlikely tool with which to intrude on some mental organizations. For example, if Sander (1976) is correct in his observations that maternal–infant interaction results in an adaptive "ecological niche" within the first ten days, then later biorhythms may be locked into the significant primary impact of this structure on later epigenesis. Klaus and Kennel (1976) go so far as to suggest that bonding in the first few hours of life is crucial to later development. Freud, Gesell, and the Jesuits at least gave us five years' leeway for structuralization and then left some room for flexible readaptation. If structure takes place earlier and in the preverbal period, then relative rigidity of organization may lead to poor self-organizations, lowered self-esteem, and, most significant to this discussion, deficient or diminished accessibility to incursion by verbal therapeutic techniques.

Although we have spent some time in discussing the possible source of structuralization (such as weakness or deficient biological structure, or environmental stress or caretaker–infant mishap) it nevertheless is still obscure. Moreover, we do not as yet know whether verbal linguistic forms can influence early organizations. Therapists who treat patients claim some success using words, but we are often told that the quality of the process and the relationship must be altered. Indeed, the models are frequently less interpretatively insight-oriented and more relational.

The stated arguments about the possible intrinsic ego factors in maladaptive character structures are more biopsychological than those of Lacan, the psychoanalyst who is most identified with structuralism. Lacan (1956), in a departure from the mainstream of psychoanalytic thinking, presented what many think of as a rather obtuse and difficult system but one which rested heavily on linguistics and structuralism. Like the structural linguists, he approached the text prior to the organism and insisted on a radical rereading of Freud to discover the meaning that others (his psychoanalytic colleagues) destroyed by theory building and change. He took his impetus, interestingly enough, from such central linguistic thinkers as Jakobson, who, among other achievements, described with Halle a number of binary oppositions wihin linguistic structures (Jakobson, Fant, & Halle, 1969). The most complete of these descriptive theories concerned phonetic and the metaphoric-metonymic poles whose features enable us to understand the structure and organization of language. Lacan used the contrast between a *metaphoric* pole, which deals with relations of similarity and substitution, and a *metonymic* pole, which draws on the laws of contiguity and connection. These are tendencies of mind and may be revealed in one individual or in another in varying proportion to emerge as external signs of character organization. We should recognize in these polar concepts Freud's mechanism of condensation and displacement which he thought of as energic shifts or primary process. These shifts, however, were used to describe the emergent resultant thoughts rather than character organizations.

Of greater significance in Lacan's model is the notion that the unconscious is a structure to be discovered and interpreted. If this is the case, the therapeutic auditor is constantly provided with a second-level message which is the result of a symbolic transformation, and the unconscious "deep structure" must be decoded. Thus, a symptom is not a sign of a disorder, but a message coded according to rules and transformations appropriate to what Lacan calls the "discourse of the other." These are unconscious structural organizations. For Lacan, the unconscious is a language itself to be interpreted and understood. In fact, the whole process of Lacanian analysis is one of exegesis of an individual's unconscious mental organization. Indeed, every ritual and myth may be looked at in the same light, and, in that sense, one may discern not only Lacan's relationship to Freud but also to Lévi-Strauss. In the most extreme sense, the analyst may be interpreting his own unconscious because it and its countertransferential trends provide the limit of his understanding another. Major (1977), a French analyst influenced to some degree by Lacan, has recently written a volume (the title roughly translates as *To Dream the Other*) which offers some insight into the structural idealism implied in this point of view. Freud's distinction between reconstruction and construction provided an interesting departure for this school: if what is told to a patient in words was experienced, we are jogging the memory. However, if a construction is a creation of the analysis in words, we are verbalizing a structure of mind in as close an approximation as words will permit. The latter may be nothing more than a rewording of a universal fantasy, but to be registered effectively, it must be timed to the patient's receptivity and not be jarring to his appreciation of his own experience (cf. Wilson, 1978).

The method as described is distinctly mentalistic and nonempirical as is the quest for competence in linguistics. The approach is to find the truth behind the appearances, not to find the appearances and then order them into truths. It is deductive.

Lacan proceeded to describe an analogue concept the "development of the eye" which mirrors the external world in what he called an "imaginary order," including all the imagery of an individual. Thus, the concept of eye is not an isolating concept of a solipsistic receiver but a concept of the relationship between the self and the world around. In this sense, we see a parallel to Kohut's idea concerning the development of self-systems out of complicated, early identificatory processes. Moreover, Loewald's (1970) idea that we internalize experience with others and not objects seems to be similarly congruent. Without going further into Lacan's complex ideas, I would like to explore how we might apply some of the notions of linguistic structure to character structure and how we might use language as an observable organization to understand the difficult circumstances of discourse with others and with ourselves.

If one were to look at the exploratory therapeutic process as a continuing dyadic relationship over a prolonged period of time, during which a number of relational dynamisms become exposed and examined, then one would have a proposition which overlaps not only Freud's but also Sullivan's view of process in therapy. Freud believed that the distortions that emerged as he was trying to discover the contents of unconscious organizations were played out on the analyst as a neutral mirror. Sullivan (1953), on the other hand, felt that the relationship itself might be utilized to explicate what he refered to as the *prototaxic* or *parataxic distortions* from the past and from the emergent distortions within the present. At any rate, if one were to accept the developmental point of view and the molding role of a series of significant relationships from the earliest years of life, which are reflected in the relationship to the therapist, one ought to find the elements of those relationships emerging insistently in some fragmented way in the therapy. One or another of the earlier relationships should predominate at varying times during the therapy. We talk about mother transference and father transference but in our global personality organization we are only, more or less, like one of our parents. We are not exact replicas or clones. As such, at any one time, the relationship to the therapist may seem to the patient to take on certain aspects of one or another of his early relationships which when analyzed into words by the therapist is registered in consciousness.

The individual patient must then look at what has been described. He must determine if the described distortion of perception has the ring of truth, and is useful to explain the nature of his feelings toward the therapist. This makes therapy a series of confrontations in words with the parts of one's psyche as revived in the tragedies and comedies that emerge in interaction with the analyst. As such, each individual is to be viewed as an amalgam of his past relevant experiences. However, that which makes it an amalgam is not something derived only from the relationship itself but also from the intrinsic structuralizing propensities of the synthesizing function of the ego. The integrative aspects of the central nervous system surely play a role, too, but only as the substrate for psychic synthesis. Moreover, our genetic propensity to emerge like our parents also plays a role in determining how much we will interact with our caretakers to emerge with traits that are either like theirs or in reaction to theirs. Suffice it to say that in normal development the process of forming a structural identity does not involve internalizing our caretakers as wholes. The wholeness of our characters are emergent from sequence upon sequence of small bits of experience with others (sometimes repeated), interacting with a variety of states of mind experienced as needs or arousals, or rage and love, or indifference. We thus become somewhat like but never the same as another. The mind is in a continuous creative synthesis of the raw material of our genetic unfolding and our percepts.

The Oedipus complex, described by Freud, may be regarded as one of the most significant hierarchic reorganizations in a long chain of hierarchic shifts. Both biodevelopmental and psychic reasons accrue as significant for this new structure (Shapiro, 1977a). Whatever enters into the Oedipus complex as a possibility creates a psychological description in formal terms of that organization which determines later behaviors. Recognition of the complex enables us to define the varied permutations and combinations of relationship with others that appear later in life. It is a good description of the phenomenology of human difficulty and help seeking in a formula that has a kinship with Chomsky's cry for a study of competence. The Oedipus complex offers deep structural slots into which the casting director of life inserts the characters, and, in this sense, it is a structure with many transformational potentials.

In psychoses, we see purer culture examples of paranoid projection of whole individuals rather than the synthetic amalgams noted in normal structures. Similarly, in studies of psychotic children, it is quite clear that they seem to take in the environment whole (Shapiro, Huebner, & Campbell, 1974). Introjected objects talk to these children from within with hallucinated clarity. Kernberg's (1977a) splitting mechanism also describes a rather archaic internal organization of objects in a structure based on a good-bad binary feature analysis that has a structural base.

These elements of varying levels of psychic structure ought to be visible in the speech of the patient. That speech pattern may then be used as the reflection of the language organization of the patient which could be seen as the best observable structural indicator of the personality itself. What I am suggesting is that linguistic behavior (speech, prosody, gestural, mimetic components and other communicational organizations) could be studied to reflect not only the structural organization of unconscious fantasies to be revealed, but also to give the therapist an external clue from which he may build up an image of the patient at varying stages in the therapy. These clues, in turn, offer a glimpse of significant relational structuring during a patient's development.

To explicate the use of language style and structure as a window to such inner structures, let me introduce a few clinical observations wherein structural wholes are available for observation and from which we may infer transformations that led to the external structures. What appears in behavior as choices may have been requirements of developmental organization that show up inadvertently as ego syntonic speech and language styles and structures. We know they are inadvertent because when the patient is confronted, he may deny or acknowledge the trait but can rarely tell us from whence it came or how it emerged without further analysis.

As an example, let me cite the case of a patient who continually referred to his mother as "the mother" or to parts of his body as "the penis" or "the head." A patient who does this is denying his closeness or attachment to even such intimate objects as the parts of his body. His language "choice," which amounts to preference in usage of definite articles, is not a usual cultural variant but rather a reflection of a character style which is idiosyncratic. This example of speech behavior may be a sign of distancing from those most intimate aspects of his object world and body image. As therapists we suspect that this entails an isolation of affect, obsessional character structures, and other concomitant behaviors. When such structural entailments are extreme, the definite article may reflect even more significant castration and separation anxiety than is dealt with by what amounts to denial mechanisms that evolve into reality dystonic behavior. After all "the penis" may be dealt with as indifferently as "the candlestick"—to be stored away and only polished for company. The implied denial of affective charge is served by such behavior as well and keeps such an individual from close human ties that tax his capacity to tolerate his internal objects.

Our language productions convey these dimensions of affective removal not only in prosody or gesture but also in the shift to formalisms. The warding off of transference that such patter signifies needs only to be mentioned. Technically, it might be expected that the therapist will have to remind the patient of his emerging feelings toward him and follow up this confrontation with an interpretation of the nature of those feelings and what primitive and archaic fantasies are thought to be warded off.

Kernberg (1977b) examined similar matters in what he called a structural diagnosis of the borderline. He directed us to look for a lack of integrated identity and evidence of "identity diffusion" which would be apparent in "a poorly integrated concept of the self and of significant others" (p. 103). He discussed these impressions on the basis of a "subjective experience of chronic emptiness, contradictory self-perceptions, contradictory behavior, that cannot be integrated in an emotionally meaningful way, and shallow, flat, impoverished perceptions of others" (p. 103). Moreover, he suggested that there might be a continuum of defensive operations which center around primitive organizations such as splitting; that is, primitive idealization and devaluation of the therapist. More abrupt shifts in representation of the therapist than one might envisage are frequent occurrences. In addition, projection and projective identification should be predominant in the defensive operations in which one's unpleasant impulses are seen in the therapist and responded to with fear, and the corresponding need is to control the other person for fear of being the recipient of the warded-off impulses.

It is possible that these behaviors might appear as transformations in linguistic forms. Indeed, there are a group of patients who have been designated as "As if" characters who correspond to the current terminology of borderline. They pick up the accents, tonal qualities, and general structural appearance of the language performance and speech of those with whom they are transiently identified. Although some professionals suggest that adolescence is a time of life when such transient identifications are normal, one may find them operative well into adulthood, in the borderline as transient processes of incorporation, in the service of self-regulation, and in relation to the idealized object that is being emulated. These transformations serve as a means of building self-esteem on the basis of being the same as the object that is idealized. However, the transience of such structures is to be divined from history as well as a sense of superficiality, shallowness, and falseness. The examiner's sense that these are transient structures also comes from the rapid fluctuation over a period of time as he sees shifts from one form of identification to another.

As previously noted, Rosen (1966) wrote about patients who speak about people they know as though there were no separation between the examiner and themselves. Their referential system does not demand any further explanation than just saying that "Johnny" said such and such—the expectation being that the examiner like the patient himself would naturally know who Johnny is and for what he stands. The idea that we share a basic reality as human beings is extended to the notion that without further intimate knowledge of each other, there is no private barrier or distinction between personal private knowledge and public knowledge. The mistaken judgment of individuals with such borderline identity organizations is that, because we speak a common language, we have a common store of understanding of each other. Such patients usually have the basic linguistic structure to carry on conversations just as the therapist does, but they organize these linguistic structures into specific affective speech patterns which are largely imitative—but so well mimicked that they mistake them for their own and do not feel these patterns to be ego dystonic. The examiner's difficulty in empathizing with such persons should serve as a clue that what is being reflected in the overt behavior is not a true amalgam of experiences appearing as a personal continuity and a sense of wholeness within the individual examined, but is rather the outcome of recent and current transforms.

Although these structural indicators might be discernible even within an initial interview, they are more likely to emerge as the therapist becomes increasingly familiar with the person. During the course of a classical analysis, one may see similar regressions in form as the patient describes his human relationships and as anxiety emerges. Regressions in form may appear as language simplifications—talking baby talk when in the throes of embarrassment, assuming the accent of other members of the family, or lapsing into foreignisms. These are most evident as the reliving in the transference begins to take place. This "reexperiencing" affords the therapist an opportunity to point to these behaviors as evidence of the impact of the past on current relationships and provides a specific observable behavior that both the analyst and the observing ego of the patient can view together to decipher the meaning of what is being said, not in conventional reference but in terms of idiosyncratic references. Thus, the reliving via archaic linguistic forms may become the stuff of analysis. This does not preclude the fact that content analysis itself may also be relevant, but the resistance may appear in the form of productions and may also be understood and analyzed as a means of getting at the anxiety which is part of the varying behaviors that emerge.

Requesting free association from patients or offering an open-ended possibility for history taking provides the analyst with a specific data base. The naturally occurring historical facts offer a different kind of organic synthesis that is dictated by the patient in talking to the therapist, rather than the history that is elicited by specific questions (Schafer, 1978a). We notice not only what is omitted and who in the family or among friends is not mentioned. Indeed, there is an easy rule of thumb that the unmentioned parent in a history of this sort may be the very parent who is the major object of identification. From a structural vantage point, there is no need to mention the parent because the potential patient represents that parent by his or her actual style, pattern, and presentation.

In summary, one might approach a patient's discursive manner from the standpoint of a linguistic pattern which has the wholeness of a structure that parallels the structural organization of the personality itself. The individual presents as a whole person with a whole story to tell—organized with a style that is as much an object of psychiatric scrutiny as the content of that story. These initial observations of linguistic patterning become an important parameter for future work with the patient because they point not only to the structural oganization of the personality but also to the habitual use of certain transformations that constitute the habitual style of presentation.

11

Talking to Children and Adolescents

One can see how many times patients have failed to convey a sense of self because a therapist has interpreted a snake as a penis symbol.

—D. W. Winnicott, 1971, p. 10.

Child therapists frequently admonish their supervisees to speak at the level of the child. Surely, this does not signify that one speak with the speech of the child, but rather at the level of the child's linguistic competence and ability to grasp what is being said. Thus, the words and grammatical structures that we use ought to coincide as closely as possible with the child's general cognitive abilities and the actual lexicon that he or she uses. Indeed, this might well be considered a general dictum in adult therapy. Significantly, the impact of using a patient's own words as opposed to using an alien vocabulary is manifestly effective. We certainly should avoid speaking to patients in metapsychological terms or in the argot of our particular theoretical framework. So why should we use one of the many pretentious codes unless our aim is to further distance us. Instead, we should substitute for classic Latinisms the lingua franca that dominates the therapeutic milieu. Furthermore, since the patient should be doing most of the talking, it ought to be his brand of lingua franca. This task becomes even more controversial when we deal with age-stage related abilities of children and especially those of adolescents wherein the particular variations in linguistic performance characterizing that stage confound our comprehension still more.

Talking to preschool children in which the dominant activity in the therapeutic session involves play requires the largest modification in technique. The therapist does well to begin with designating the activities carried out by the youngster in his play behavior. The child is confronted naturally with the naming-describing function with which he is familiar. He also gets the idea that doing is complemented by saying and that saying is an aim of the interaction. We will examine a series of descriptions concerning the play and the action that is called forth in the play.

The tendency for nursery teachers and therapists to use the present progressive tense is well worth noting insofar as the /-ing/ ending of that tense dominates the linguistic activities heard during such interactions: "Jimmy is *playing* with a block" or "Jimmy is *building* a castle" or "He's *putting* mommy in the castle and now *knocking* the castle over." The next step after such descriptions in the present progressive tense usually involves a semi-interpretative remark that recognizes a wish, a motivation, or, in young children, the beginnings of designating affects is opposed to acting upon them: "Jimmy is angry at his mommy." If this response is to the negative, then one might begin to point again to the play: "The blocks and the castle did tumble down about her?"

The latter confrontational exchange is stated without using a /wh/ phrase—what, when, who, where—which tend to be rather confusing and poorly understood by young children. Since they learn these pro-forms (substitutes for nouns or pronouns) somewhat later, the earlier period of confrontation ought to exclude /wh/ forms. Moreover, the promiscuous use of the /wh/ form is taken by young children as an accusation especially in the word *why*. This is because the young child has so often heard the word *why* following a minor misdemeanor in which a parent has said "Why did you do that?" or "What did you do?" The intention of the therapeutic intervention is to bring a behavior under the ego's control and not to serve as an anlage for superego chastisement.

As we consider the possibilities of being able to make more than confrontations to children and which terms in what language to use, we must try to find a way to convey intrapsychic conflict without confusion. To do this, we have to state the conflict in terms that the child can deal with himself. In the simplest language of the child, it might be best to state two opposing wishes back to back, rather than saying "You are conflicted by," or to state an apposition. For example, the therapist might say "You want to go, but you also want to stay"—or if the *but* seems too advanced—"You want to go, and you want to stay" adding the general clarifier "both at the same time," if he can take a sentence of that length. Children with attentional deficits might not. Moreover, children with nagging parents turn off after two words. Laconism wins that session not loquatiousness. One can easily move toward an affect following such a statement by saying "and that makes you feel fidgety in your hands" or "restless so you run around" or "worried inside." Each of these statements places the feeling state closer to a cognitive concept moving first from an observable body state that can be called by name.

As we discuss the matter of talking to children, it becomes clear that one of the tasks in the therapy of youngsters concerns the linking of behavior, qua activity, with their verbalizations to state what we generally call *affects* or *feeling states*. For the most part, preschool children have not learned to designate the nuances of feeling and less frequently to equate them with situational circumstances in which anticipation and control become possible if the linkage is appreciated. One of the earliest tasks in therapy with young children and even older children who have not been exposed to the nuances of language is to teach the words that match their feelings and how they relate to the situation that gives rise to such varied body and mind states. For example, "You do this or that when you feel Y or Z." "You knock over blocks when you feel worried that I am going to say 'no' to you." "You always become quiet and silent and stop playing when you feel angry." "You are afraid that I will punish you for doing an angry thing." "Oh, your daddy went away! That feeling you have which makes you want to cry while you're holding back the tears is called sadness." You may wish to offer the possibility and sense of the universality of feeling by sad by saying "and everybody feels that way when somebody who is loved has gone off." This may seem didactic rather than analytic but it represents a significant step in making what seems private, public or what seems magical and isolated, social.

Teaching the names of affects is only part of the story, because these affects must be linked to ideational and situational content or else the names remain dangling as designations of mental states devoid of content and devoid of anticipatory power, to be called forth when certain circumstances recur in the life of the child. The aim of therapeutic connunication with children as with adults concerns the possibility of offering a verbal lexical vehicle by which he or she can designate what used to be an unknown mysterious thing and change it to a current familiar thing that can be rendered less overwhelming.

There are two difficult problems in interpreting the unconscious to a child: the first concerns the tendency to turn the unconscious into an out-of-awareness, out-of-control animus that permits lack of responsibility; the second concerns his or her cognitive and linguistic capacity to comprehend that current behaviors may be dictated by prior patterns and prior experiences. The therapist has to be sure that the child understands such phrases as "when you remember" or "the difference between before and after" which are linguistic forms that are arrived at somewhat late, compared to the early lexical ability to designate the here and now (Harner, 1976; Miller, 1977). For this reason, we often stick to the description of the play activity on displaced objects and discuss affects, feelings, and inner conflict states in terms of play material, prior to bringing it home in relation to the past and current life situation or in the transference. If language is to serve as a scaffolding for ideation, it is the scaffolding which links the past with the present and the present with the behavior of the child in the therapeutic situation, either as a current reality or as a transferential phenomenon.

As the therapist advances toward the period of latency and the stage of concrete operations, the child also has a better grasp of nuances of grammar and lexical possibilities exemplified by his understanding the passive voice phrases or the flow of elements from the past into the present. Even the mastery of sequences such as days of the week bodes well for linguistic grasp. One might even suggest that latency signifies a significant cognitive event as well as a dynamic event (Shapiro & Perry, 1976) in which one clearly has to work with the unconscious as well as the conscious activities. Repression is more clearly evident and obsessive rigor has covered over the linguistic charm of earlier phrases and phases. However, although children of this stage have achieved a good deal of comprehensional ability, they are still not in the stage of abstract operational thought. As such, the therapist not only has to continue to speak in their language, choosing vocabulary carefully, but also has to speak at the complexity level that they are used to handling.

The child is much more likely to be engaged in some direct play activities or direct verbal interplay with the therapist and may even be able to bring in his or her feelings as something to talk about as well as be able to designate nuances of sadness, elation, disappointment, or rage. The tendency toward acting out in some children at this stage has to be stated very carefully in terms of fantasy activity influencing behavior—a matter which is not apparent to many adults or children. One of the most useful therapeutic activities in this period of life is to make the distinction between *thinking* and *doing* while at the same time helping the patient to see that doing is used sometimes instead of thinking about things. These dicta are already a part of the general activities of therapists who deal with adults, but must be highlighted for routine use with children. There is a tendency to undercut the importance of such distinctions by their apparent banality and to surmise that they are generally known.

Encouragement of the child that the task of the meetings is to talk about feelings and problems must be at the forefront of a therapist's activity. However, many new therapists sometimes tend to fall into what seems to them like "nagging" rather than "interpreting" behaviors. Making sure that the child understands what he is doing may also be contrary to the aims of the meetings which in the initial phases are to establish a basis for unpressured communication in which the usual demands of the day-to-day world are suspended. In the words of Anthony (1974), therapeutic space is a land "between yes and no."

While we attempt to understand, the child is at a stage of development in which his wishes may become manifest during the therapy by a series of attempted exploitations; "Will you take me for a soda?" "Let me call my mother." "Oh, can I take home this toy?" "Oh, I would love to have the magazine in your waiting room." All these wishes can be satisfied easily enough, and, indeed, at times, when one is doing ego supportive activity or work that requires some compensations for parents' neglect, one may acquiesce. Even in child analysis many analysts offer the child some nutriment, especially after a long school day, with the knowledge that a little hypoglycemia impairs the attention to the therapy. More important, there is the natural expectation that the interaction between an adult and child is such that the adult is nurturing, giving, as well as understanding. That difficult step between "what do you give" and "how much do you avoid the giving" so that the *wishing* becomes apparent as a thought is one which only the sensitivity of practice and adequate supervision can teach the therapist. In unconscious terms, what you say to the child is also nutriment and must therefore be couched in digestible terms, both sweetened and strong enough to be effective. But if we need a way to the digestive center, a pinch of originality pays off. The child all too readily falls into your locution and begins to ignore what you say and even tells you how boring your are in your repetitiousness if you lack spice in your delivery. The child patient may fail to see repetitiousness in his own play behavior as the source of why you, the therapist, are repetitious. But it is possible that the lack of color in what is said does poison the content so that the child cannot tolerate it. This brings us to the possibility of peppering one's confrontations and interpretations from early childhood on well into adolescence with a lot more of the paralinguistic and prosodic music than we may be accustomed to in adult therapy.

It is truly condescending, however, to speak to a child in the high-pitched falsetto that signifies his or her inequality with you. Most children find this offensive. On the other hand, it *is* possible to use a grammatical form which is closer to their own, while at the same time appropriately raising and lowering the pitch of your voice to show appreciation and excitement or offer encouragement in the way in which you say something. If we remember that the affective envelope of what we say is probably learned prior to the content of what we say (Stern, 1979), in being closer then to that period when words were not available to a child, we do well to maintain the affective envelope if we are to keep the therapeutic alliance and make communicational sense. Besides, there is nothing so monotonous as the "hm" or mumbling of pat analytic phrasing. Since the task of therapy with children is to bring them back into life, a little liveliness in the way in which things are said is very helpful to the child and increases his or her willingness to receive what is said.

Chronological age alone would not dictate the syntactic and lexical forms that are used. We must also know something about the intellectual capacity of those ages or the degree of psychosis which may have its secondary effect on understanding. Watch how simply the child himself speaks; there may be minor retardation. The quality of the interpretation has to follow the degree of social sophistication, too. In a similar fashion there are a group of children, some of whom are psychotic, some of whom are simply obsessional, who use a broad-range vocabulary and rather pretentious Latinisms. Although we might not want to speak in the language of an unskilled laborer to this type of child, we might make such a child understand that we grasp what he is saying by not confronting him with his pretensions but answering him in kind, without mocking. Because he becomes so accustomed to alienating himself from others by his mannerisms, it may be comforting that our speech is nonjudgmental. The look of appreciation that the therapist receives when the obesssional child is given some thing back in kind, this time with a gestural or mimetic twinkle (as well as a prosodic lilt), might be very useful in establishing contact especially in initial interviews.

Some psychotic children go so far as to create entire new languages made up of complex phonemes and morphemes and new lexicons. Strictly speaking, these are not likely to be new languages in a grammatical sense, for the syntax is rarely changed, but the new vocabulary is the focus. One suspects the referential change is in the service of shunning the things of this world. Such children are usually all too willing to share with you the nature of their supposed genius. Indeed, this is their very specialized message which says in essence "I am cut off from my peers and everyone else, but what I am looking for is a special group of people who will be able to not only admire me, but also will wish to communicate with me in kind." They also offer the challenge of meeting them more than halfway by learning a new tongue. I am suggesting that the message-carrying unit on the child's part may be simple verbalization, but, if we paid greater attention to the form as well as the content, we might be able to decipher and dissect some of the origins and intentions of the production so that the perlocutionary force of these speech acts may be interpreted in the appropriate framework, and all is not lost in the narrow focus of the words, grammar, or prosody.

Although children may not consciously speak in metaphors, it is interesting how metaphoric their speech can be. Indeed, the child's capacity for imaginary companions or the tendency to humanize a pet dog provides a useful vehicle from which one can begin to understand the nature of the individual and idiosyncratic human relations and wishes. A. A. Milne (1961) in his poem, "Binker," describes a relationship with an imaginary companion. The child in the poem suggests that Binker likes sweets and that is why "he always asks for two." One comes to a full understanding of the existence of Binker as a "talking companion" by the end of the poem, and the realization that all the adults in this child's life seem available too infrequently for this child's needs. However, his wishes are revealed via displacement to the needy companion.

Some of the sociolinguistic models are instructive with respect to how children respond to what the therapist says. We have already mentioned the tendency of children to take /wh/ questions as accusations. They also have tendencies to take other comments in an accusing, punishing way. For example, if you walked into the room and said "The window is open," it might sound like a simple description of the state of the window sash. However, if you are sitting in a room and the two of you are shivering and one of you is closest to the window, and you utter the phrase "The window is open," surely it will have the illocutionary force "Close the window!" You can imagine that the impact of such a comment would be even greater on a late latency child in the room with an adult, because it is so often the tendency in many households that the younger child as opposed to the adult is expected to do the bit of work that is required to drop the sash. Of course, the reverse might be equally possible in households where affluence is the case and "thank God, the child doesn't have to move." We can see how descriptions are sometimes turned into prescriptions by certain children.

In confronting the child, the therapist must take care and be certain it is clear in describing a state of affairs that it does not mean that the therapist necessarily wishes him or her to change, that the intention to change has to come from within, and that the choice to change is free if the wish is that certain circumstances are to be brought about. It is therefore possible with children over eight that "if . . . then" hypothetical phrases might be used as a way of conveying the possibility for change. In fact, phrases such as "Suppose you," or "Let's pretend that," or "Do you think if" might be used to introduce contrary-to-fact conditional ideas that the child might be interested in enacting. The consequences of those actions might be considered in the phrasing as described. During play sessions, one could make the easy displacement of representation from the concrete to the inner life by analogy, once one is assured that the child has preconscious grasp that the tasks embarked on concern the establishment of greater contact with his or her feelings.

Let us consider a seven-year-old child who has begun to elaborate a sequence of play with a small car. During a session, a ramp was constructed which is essentially an inclined plane that enabled the car to move from a great height on the table to the rim of the table, accelerating in speed as it fell. As the car went tumbling over the edge, the child seemed greatly excited. A simple description of the behavior might be put in terms of how fast the car goes and how excited the child feels when he sees it going so fast. Thus far, we have not breached even the austerity of a behaviorist's principles. During the next step, the child might comment, "Yes, it goes fast, but look it crashed on the bottom." It might be possible to state that "Going fast is exciting, but the danger of getting broken is a real problem." If the child then suggested that the car should have wings like "Chitty Chitty Bang Bang" so that it could convert itself into an airplane to avoid danger, one might exclaim "What a wonderful car!" Were the therapy further along, "What a wonderful car; it not only goes fast, but it can fly and doesn't have to worry about the dangers below." If we wanted to emphasize the denial implied in the wings which prevent the crash, the therapist might say "Wouldn't it be wonderful if cars had wings?" That would then put the emphasis on the fact that both therapist and child understand that this is not so, and that it is merely a wish to protect against the overwhelming aspect of the excitement leading to danger.

During the same play, the child might construct a series of barriers at the bottom of the ramp or comment, as the car came to an abrupt halt, that it had marvelous brakes. The therapist might comment "What a wonderful car to be able to go fast, and be able to stop just at the point that the danger became very great." This would emphasize both wish and defense, excitement and inhibition, and offer the child the concrete medium in which to play out and begin to work through some of the ramifications of his wishes and their dangers if executed.

The ultimate transfer of such statements about the play to the child's own emotions would have to come at an appropriate point as a description of the sense of excitement and restraint within himself, either by analogy or by demonstration in the play situation. Of, if we had gone through this sequence over and over again and knew of similar circumstances in our young patient's life, a question might broach the gap between play and life: "Wasn't that similar to this and that?" or "When you wanted to go on a roller coaster you felt so excited, and then you had to stay home with a tummyache because you were afraid that the excitement would be too much—it was like this." These verbalizations would be ways of making the linkages that are necessary in treatment so that the child's grasp of his circumstances both in play, with the therapist, and with the world he lives in could be integrated, brought together, and become a usable structure around which he could anticipate future excitement and dangers.

Genetic links to the past are a problem in child therapy because they involve a certain amount of "as if" thinking. "You act now *as if* your mother had deprived you then" represents the general form in which we find that therapists make genetic reconstructions. For the child, it must be put much more in terms of his feelings and *what* he actually remembers. Phrases such as "You remember what you told me about you and mommy when you went to the movies when you were two" or "You didn't remember what you felt, but from what you said just now, we could guess that you felt alone and sad but couldn't say it then." Thus, language even in the quite young child permits a possibility for stating how the facts of your observations cohere with the facts that you are aware of in his or her life. Winnicott's book, *The Piggle* (1977), provides a number of examples of genetic interpretation to a very young patient and the degree of imagination necessary to grasp the meaning of play data. The linkages to knowledge of current life and concerns are essential.

Talking to adolescents provides another set of problems and also some of the same problems we have when talking to young children. We might begin by classifying the problems of talking to adolescents not in terms of the biology of their developmental stage but, more importantly, in terms of their sociology. If we were to draw a systems diagram of adolescence, it would be best represented by that overlapping space in which childhood and adulthood intersect. Whatever rite of passage each culture offers adolescents to mark his or her march into this period, there are no formal rites of passage which involve the introduction of a secret language that arises naturally. And yet, adolescence, with its sociology of gang formation, chumship, and new group arrangements, creates a situation in which linguistic drift and usage take on a unique form. This has occurred during every stage of history. There is no period in development in which language variance from the general standard tongue spoken in the surround undergoes such rapid idiosyncratic changes. The Opies (1959) have described the language and lore of childhood in terms of the uniformity of game structure, rhyme, and jargon for latency by oral transmission. Similarly, adolescents have a network of linguistic movement which is carried by their music, their songs, and their propensity to play with language in small and secret group interchanges. The lingo of the bobby-soxer in the 1940s contrasted with the language of the "greaser" attests to the rapid shifts that take place in a brief span of 20 to 30 years.

If we begin by reiterating the notion that psychotherapy is a mutual enterprise between therapist and patient, both of whom are engaged in a quest for meaning, it is not a simple matter to discover what someone is thinking by what he says if we are not acquainted with his personal argot. This is especially so if we seek to discover the nuances of meaning that are so important to our adolescent patients who are all too prone to feel that they are misunderstood. When engaging an adolescent, we have to follow an example parallel to that of other patients. The formal code used must obey similar rules of surface structure formation and deep structural organization, for both parties to be understood. It is even more important to therapeutic encounters that the code be comprehensible, because, when we focus on the unconscious, the manifest language is a vital link to the language of that unconscious. While we reach for that language, the rules of discourse of each individual must guarantee at least potential agreement so that other levels may be reached. Indeed, as has been indicated earlier, the other levels may not be reached solely by the discourse itself, but in messages hidden in the form of the discourse and how it varies from person to person or group to group. When viewed from this vantage, a number of characteristic problems arise when talking to adolescents that may be treated linguistically. They can be subsumed under problems of interpreting the speech act and its significance, and more significantly to the quandary of reference. A set of principles about talking to adolescents should grow out of our respect for this problem. The three areas of reference that concern us during the adolescent period are linguistic drift, imprecision of usage, and adolescent argot.

Linguistic drift has been approached as a diachronic science; that is, words change in meaning and change in reference over time and geography. New words (neologisms) may even be created by cultural need as well as by individuals. When dealing with adolescents, we see a microcosmic short-term shift in meaning and lexicon at a synchronic level. Such shifts may be even more radical and sudden than longer term diachronic shifts.

Three types of drift may be noticed. The first concerns the changing meaning of the same word. A common word among adolescents during the 1970s is *fag*. By general agreement, most adolescents use the word fag to describe somebody who does not fit, who is a bit persnickety, who cannot take the rough and tumble; in short, somebody who may not be "one of the guys" or maybe a little bit outside of the group, more likely to be prim or bookish and nonsocial. In later adolescence, the homosexual significance is clearer. It was not so long ago during the 1950s and early 1960s when a *fag* uniformly referred to a homosexual, so that to be called a fag by someone in one's group not only referred to the outsider's role but also to the outsider with a specific sexual orientation. If one goes back further in history to Tom Brown's school days, it is clear that a *fag* was somebody who did menial tasks for an upperclassman at school and became fatigued or fagged out. He was in no way looked upon as a homosexual except insofar as there was a sadomasochistic aspect to the same-sex relationship that might be attributable to features of both designata. There is also an additional common use of *fag* which may be detected from context. For example, in passing a cigarette an adolescent might say "Pass the fag." Tracing the etymological history further takes us to the word *fagot* or *faggot*; *fag* derives from the word *fagot*, which refers to the bundle of twigs that was carried in the original *fasces* during the time of the Latin beginnings of our language. There is also a Greek equivalent *phakelos*. The word *fag* has had important designative significance since then, but a meaning quite far from current adolescent usage. It is curious that currently to call somebody a faggot rather than a fag again refers back to the homosexual aspect of its various meanings when used by an adolescent. Linguistic drift is also evident in phrases as well as words.

Phrases such as "going out" in the terminology of the 1940s and 1950s referred to the fact that an adolescent was seeing someone on a single date, or possibly more than one date, but not with serious intentions. Currently, it is the rough equivalent of what adolescents of the 1940s called "going steady" and adolescents in the 1920s referred to as "keeping company." Similarly, "making out" might refer to kissing and petting, but certainly not to coitus these days; in former years, it might have referred to all three. The newly invented phrase "getting on over somebody" involves the ultimate aim of the foreplay referred to. "First, second, third, and home base" are not only used to designate the male adolescent's preoccupation with baseball but also his anatomical interest in a female conquest when he describes the progress of his sexual victory.

There is a phrase drift, too, that occurs in the opposite direction, that is, from the figurative to the literal. "We slept together" is one such example. It might currently mean nothing more than that; specifically, the act of being in a somnolent state in the same bed with somebody. In former years, it was a euphemism for coital interaction. Recent adolescent terminology also borrows heavily from psychiatric discipline. Somebody might say "I got crazy" and mean "I became excited" or say "He's paranoid" and not be referring to a fullblown psychiatric state but rather the idea of becoming suspicious, especially when under the influence of marijuana. Thus, we have to adjust our receptive understanding so that we do not confuse the same reference as having a constant referent when talking to an adolescent. That which is usually signified may be quite different in the language of the adolescent. Moreover, he or she may be carrying it to you in just that way in order to confuse rather than to inform, or to test your understanding of adolescents as a group. This brings us to Freud's important discovery in the interpretation of dreams; that we dare not use standard symbol translation to interpret dreams. The individual associations and the context of the dream are more importnat to on-target understanding. The caution is similarly important in understanding the language of the adolescent.

The second feature of adolescent usage is its imprecision. One example of a problem that arises comes directly from the popularity of psychological thinking in our time, especially that focused on Erik Erikson's view of identity. The anomie of the twentieth century is translated by the intellectual adolescent into "I don't know who I am." Therapists dare not look at statements such as that, as comments that do not need translation into the language of the unconscious. The simple answer to "I don't know who I am" is "Your are what you do." This may sound too pragmatic and operational to satisfy the troubled youngster, but it clearly shifts focus from the abstract to the action–self. The philosophical implication of "I don't know who I am" seems to stem from the romantic interest of young adolescents in the books of Hermann Hesse, or of Buddhism, transcendental meditation, and mysticism. Psychologically, such problems may be better described in the language of Mahler concerning merging, as-if personality, and identity formation. They may correspond to trendy conversations and be reflections or residues of conversations that adolescents have with other adolescents rather than true pictures of what is in reality the inner state. This wish for immediacy also corresponds to the protest implied in "I gotta use words when I talk to you," when the adolescent in the psychotherapeutic process finds that he has to move toward the therapist by using his language, instead of the therapist moving toward the adolescent with his language.

A second area of imprecision comes from the problem of defining feelings. General statements such as "I feel upset" or the popular use of "being uptight" reflect a vagueness which serves a defensive purpose for the adolescent by claiming ignorance of the nuances of feelings in relation to ideas. The therapist in that instance must break through the vagueness and introduce the possibility of greater precision as a means of "teaching" control and anticipation and those aspects of ego mastery with which the adolescent would feel better were he not so much victimized by his own feelings. Indeed, the vagueness may hide a myriad of fantasies which he believes might make him feel even more upset or uptight were he to confront them. Imprecision is further ensconced within our language in such locutions as "you know" or "like man" which become continuing verbal confessions of the uncertainty of the adolescent's verbal skill in conveying his feelings and/or ideas. They reveal a technique in code which is continuous with the secret codes of latency and are reflected in an identification with subgroups that ensures a lack of hope for contact with the larger group—especially with those individuals who are over 30.

The latter issue brings us into the homeground of adolescent language—his argot. "I dig my head better when I'm on grass." "After all the shit has gone down, I've gotta cover my ass, because I was sure he was gonna lay it on me." What could possibly be the meaning of these phrases? They certainly correspond closely to the syntax of English, but the lexical items are used in an unusual manner. The references are different than those that usually come to mind. They sound very much like Chomsky's "colorless green ideas sleep furiously." Perhaps there are two languages: yours–mine, and the language of my people. These languages are continuous with the code of 7- to 10-year-old children and the secret social clubs of that age period. The codes are colorful, too, and function to keep these children separate from adults, almost like a new ethnic group. The newer trends reveal an identification of adolescents with subcultures that usually have been considered to be outside upper- and middle-class white communities. The modern adolescent dresses in inexpensive blue jeans designed for work, and they sport patches over their holey trousers to identify with the idea of what poor people and blacks must tolerate. In their language, too, they have tried out the phraseology which belongs to the language of these varied groups. The adolescent style also treads a rather narrow line between condescension and arrogance. He tests the therapist for his bilingualism. He asks in innumerable ways to see whether he will be understood if he uses his own language, and he always tempts the therapist to inquire if he is understood. The fact is that the therapist does have to make an adaptation to the new language, and these adaptations require a certain amount of technical skill and extra understanding if communication is to be established. Some of this technical skill and understanding may come from prior knowledge of the linguistic form that the adolescent uses.

The first general rule therapists must cherish in talking to the adolescent concerns keeping the quest for meaning at the forefront. Discussion about "speaking the same language" may then be looked at in terms of how to approach a translation rather than adopting the adolescent's style. The therapist must beware of frightening the adolescent by what he says. Because of the average clinician's imprecise knowledge of his patient's language, he may make wrong interpretations because he uses his patient's words incorrectly. He then seems like another "somebody" who does not understand. The excessive zeal of new therapists sometimes makes them talk too much or talk in a way that parallels the adolescent's patter. Homosexual fantasies of intrusiveness, of being too much at the patient's level may confound communication. Instead of meaning Y, the adolescent means X. In fact, one of the important things to be established is that our jargon is not his, and his jargon is not ours; we are in somewhat separate worlds, but they can be bridged via a slow process of talking together. An old saw in clinical work is worth mentioning at this juncture. When a patient asks whether the therapist saw a movie or read a particular book, the response should be the same. "Even if I did see (or read) it, I'd like to know what you thought of it and how you thought of it and how you saw the story from a personal vantage." Communication should and need not imply merging and loss of separateness. Pluralism is tolerable. Translation assumes work to bind people. While acknowledging that his thoughts are personal and only yielded up on an act of volition, the therapist provides a space in which such voluntary discussions are possible.

Another technical rule concerns the information-seeking mode "Why did you say that?" or "How come you said it in that way, when you talk another way usually?" Generally a shift in mode of expression might indicate a shift in significance, and the formal change addresses the particular content at that moment. It might be best to hold one's fire—to listen—and see if the content fits the form. The lisping baby talk may be regressive, but it might also be flirtations. The high-flown language may be defensive when threatened and not simply arrogant. Similarly, one must take extra care when making a confrontation to adolescents. For example, comments such as "While you're talking, you're sitting in such a way that shows me you intend to be seductive" can lead to extreme guilt and the feeling of being accused. Such a sequence frequently leads to a variety of action which carries the message "If I'm going to be hung for a lamb, I might as well be hung for a fox." "I might as well do that of which I am accused." It is important that the language of the therapist be not only appropriately timed but issued with the tact required for somebody both in the role of the compatriot as well as the potential object of a strong transference. Frequently, patients in this age group will deal not only with confrontations but also with descriptions of their behavior as permission for activity—the description that becomes the prescription mentioned so often represents the favorite distortion of adolescents in therapy.

Another factor to be considered in our adaptation of the adolescent's language is that our street language may not be seen as comraderie, but as a lie. We have to be careful that this lie does not alienate the adolescent completely from activity of exploring his unconscious or even his conscious behavior. There is a way to talk to adolescents at their level in our own words even though not in their argot. If we take up his argot, it demonstrates his power control over us. We become passive and unable to help and also open to the same ridicule and self-accusations that the adolescent may feel about himself. They may even meet us with the same condescension that is projected onto their own group. If we wish to be "let in" on the adolescent's world, we must use the same general rule of respect as used with other patients.

Although attempts at understanding and translation and striving for specificity are used universally with adolescents as with adults and younger children, nothing has been said, as yet, about the nonverbal or empathic aspects of discourse with adolescents. Empathy should be apparent in our mode of listening, our facial expression, our gestural and mimetic sympathies, and our paralinguistic tones. There is, to be sure, a complementary set of activities that occur in therapy which may be grasped while we listen, but each particular performance requires a general linguistic competence that we assume both therapist and adolescent carry.

In general, I would doubt that the formalisms of adolescent language differ very much in their structure and organization from that of the species-specific community of languages. If we were to subject adolescent language to the Whorf–Sapir hypothesis of linguistic relativity, we would examine the sociolinguistic structure of adolescence in terms of how noun, verb, and object were arranged and the variety of choices that were made around the specific word options or the idiosyncracy of linguistic form. Although each of these sectors may be translated point-by-point into any other language, there are special nuances created by adolescent idiolects which make of their words more than simple labels. They are labels which carry affectful, secret things that point to important inner concerns, as, for example, the proliferation of names for the genitals. The speech act and pragmatic frame of reference apply to adolescent language as they do to any other delivery or communication system. The problem ought to be studied as one would study a subculture with its idiosyncratic social control rules. To be an adolescent psychiatrist and listen to adolescent language is to be more expert than others in a variety of communicational modes which are subject to rapid change and continually created new forms. Vigilance to such change keeps us in a rapidly changing inner circle of great variety from social class to social class but also from day to day, from one school to another.

Psychotherapy and Psycholinguistics

Music rationalizes sound, but a more momentous rationalization of sound is seen in language.

—George Santayana, 1954, p. 325.

Because of the personal contract between patient and therapist, psychotherapy remains somewhat closed to public vision. Dyadic psychotherapies have even fewer observers than group therapies. This established privacy results in the tendency of therapists to use the humanness of their personalities to a greater degree than in any other applied science. Although the rules for the conduct of a therapy may be well prescribed as they are in psychoanalytic therapy, these rules may be altered in order to accommodate a particular therapist's artfulness. The artfulness, in turn, is said to derive from an attempt to respond empathically to perceived needs of patients. However, the distinction between the art and science of psychotherapy is trivial and misleading, because a scientific attitude toward data includes the examination of all varieties of investigation and social discourse—even that which is artful. Thus, we do not take away from that which is artful in psychotherapy by examining systematically what therapists do. Furthermore, we may use such systematic knowledge for furthering the science of what is mutative in the psychotherapeutic exchange. Without such examination we submit to mystification rather than the pursuit of rational explanation. Socrates was right, however, in suggesting that it is neither science nor art that is at the top of the heap. As both scientists and artists, psychotherapists may rest easy if they yield to philosophy the job of examining the presuppositions of both human enterprises. I, for one, gladly yield o philosophy (the love of truth) the "high place" at the table, especially if new light may be shed on the process. Linguistics is close to philosophy in examining the presuppositions and bases of verbal exchange and may serve as well.

The art does lead to a general tendency of psychotherapists to emit a "don't tread on me" attitude. Nevertheless, systematic investigations have been made which tell us something about what goes on in the dual interchange in the consulting rooms. Even Freud has had patient observers who recorded their experiences. They range from adulation (Doolittle, 1956) to acrimony (Wortis, 1954). One clear proposition that emerges from most studies is that psychotherapy is best looked at as a process rather than as a static event. Moreover, while psychotherapy is taught in texts, progressive supervision is the best way therapists have of transmitting their body of knowledge between the generations. This oral transmission is designed to accommodate the changing relationship and the unfolding nuances of meaning as they emerge between patient and therapist. However, it is generally agreed that it is the supervisee who is supervised or "controlled" and not the "case" as seen.

For our purposes, it is necessary to emphasize that both the supervisee and the "case" gain audience to the supervisor via a verbal filter. Unlike the situation in many other sciences, the facts that are examined are not statements about the phenomena observed, but the text is the summary of events reported by the therapist observer and reconstituted in the supervisory discourse with the supervisor. All of the foregoing involve a complex transfer of words and images screened as global impressions and presented as specific incidents which are cast into linguistic patterns. The presentation to a supervisor is aimed toward understanding the patient better in terms of an analytic vision. However, the supervisee has selected the vision to be presented, and the supervisor responds to this version of the reported interaction by attempting to help the therapist understand what may then be conveyed verbally to the patient. Words are again the medium and the presumption is that new information and novel formulations will be derived from those words so that the supervisee can again recaste the knowledge into words suitable for transmission to his patient. This description of the gap between "primary data" and their verbal recording should put us in mind of the idealist dictum to study man's categorizing functions, rather than his illusory nature, as a something out there.

The events of the therapeutic process to be understood and interpreted have already been analogized to the naming process. Moreover, dynamic psychotherapists, following Freud, have adopted the rule of overdetermination and its later refinements by Waelder (1936), who complemented our theory with the notion of multiple function. This latter theoretical advance still permits that there is likely a "right interpretation" at a certain point in time in the process if all data were available. Polysemanticity does not undercut the possibility that the image presented for interpretation occurs in a specific context with a single most correct meaning to be elucidated at that specific moment. In addition, this specific interpretation, even when correct, is most felicitous when given to the patient in words that are useful for understanding his behavior and not in words that add only to defensive intellectualization. Thus, the level of discourse as well as the correct designation is important for impact on the process.

Some therapists (Pine, 1976) have suggested that the therapeutic process parallels aspects of the separation–individuation process even in its interpretive mode. Spitz (1959) claimed that language onset holds central significance as the third organizer of development. Mahler, Pine, & Bergman (1975) looked at language in the separation–individuation process as instrumental in creating a special pocket of maternal reserve that can be called upon for refueling from within—even in the absence of the parent. The inbuilt capacity to develop language permits the developing child to make continuous inner restatements about the world as experienced. These inner statements are continually revised in ever subtle ways that permit reevaluation of that experience and reintegration of aspects of one's attitudes toward that experience. The accretions in ego that result become the groundstuff on which the self may be established as a separate integrated system apart from one's caretaker. The psychotherapeutic process aims at a similar goal of firm self-integration and reality oriented ego adaptation.

As the therapist talks to his patient, repeatedly offering him new formulations in words around which he may alter his inner dialogue and build his life along more adaptive behaviors, he facilitates the process described. Thus, we might say that psychotherapy utilizes the tendency to store dialogue as a means of modulating experience with significant others in the service of ego modulation. Freud's formulation of the ego as a precipitate of experience allows that agency of the mind to serve as the mediator between moral forces within the superego, and the wish for immediate gratification of wishes derived from the drives. This modulation paradoxically involves not only control of drives and satisfaction of superego forces but also the attainment of the maximum pleasure possible for the individual, in light of all the forces exerting pressure within the structure of the psyche and the demands of reality as well.

In the most primitive sense, the patient "takes in" the therapist's words under the apt conditions of the therapy. The transference readiness of the patient also provides an apt context appropriate for accepting the therapist-as-giver. Using the oral mode and zone, the therapist's words are assimilated as nutriments that achieve congruence with the earliest childhood experiences with nurturing parents. The symbolic appreciation of the words as a referential code to be assimilated rationally is a hoped for second-level experience. It may seem paradoxical to suggest that words are designed to elicit rational response, but within the context of the level of contact between patient and therapist, the latter situation may prevail, allowing only for appreciation of giving with little attention to what is given, that is, the words are lost to the music. On the other hand, when the therapist is able to hit the cognitive mark sharply and strike an appropriate congruence between what is said and what the patient experiences, the sentence expressed constitutes an illocutionary force worthy of being called a *therapeutic intervention*. The perlocutionary impact or meaningful comprehension by the patient allows for the words to impact as a potential unit that mediates change. The words, delivered and received, must be served up each successive time with slight variation so that they almost fit into prior templates. Specifically, verbal interventions should be made with a calculated degree of novelty so that the patient is neither shocked, stunned, nor unready for what is heard. This corresponds to Kris's (1950, 1956) idea that interpretations ought be timed to correspond to when the content of the interpretation is already preconscious. Piaget's formulation that mental ailments fit into prior schemata in the process of assimilation is a similar idea. Accommodation will then be fostered with new schemata evolving as the old templates require alteration under the impact of experiential demand.

Change occurs when patients are able to select the original and creative meaning designated in the word and sentence formulations. The general capacity of language to provide a shorthand representation by inflected endings and auxiliaries of temporal relations, linking past, present, and future, enables the specific statements of therapists to be encoded in a manner which corresponds to the flux of experience at varying levels of awareness. The process of the therapy makes the statements hang together and parallels the changing experience in the therapy with a therapist who, in turn, provides a relatively stable base against which that experience is measured. This is what we mean when we say a statement or intervention is meaningful, that is, it makes sense to the individual by describing his thoughts and feelings accurately and provides a manageable capsule which contains a polysemantic content. The model bears comparison to the idea that Chomsky put forth about superficial and deep structure. If a particular deep structure under the influence of transformational rules can generate innumerable surface structures, then as therapists we can provide the patient with a summary organizer in ever changing sentences that corresponds to fewer unconscious meaning units which, in turn, bring together the patient's disparate individual experiences under one unit of expression. Derivatives are recoded by therapists as unconscious wishes that render the polysemantic field less confusing and more available for conscious recognition and anticipation.

Although the process of psychotherapy may be built on the human relationships between two people, the premise of this volume has been that the most important factor to be reckoned with in interpretive therapy is the contact between two people who are involved in transferring a series of speech acts. As Bühler (1934) noted, words take on an appeal function from the moment a mother responds regularly. In many therapies modeled after psychoanalysis, patients are listened to without responding immediately, and the appeal function is apparently sacrificed temporarily. The mutual task orientation of two people looking together at one of the dyads is substituted in order to establish a common referent for that which is being described. A common referent involves the patient learning a new code or a code similar to the therapist's with a special discourse pattern. And I do believe that those who do insight-oriented psychotherapy educate their patients to the language of their unconscious. Indeed, one of Freud's aims in having future psychoanalysts undertake didactic analyses was to permit them to have a first-hand experience with their own unconscious without learning the language of metapsychology or the technical jargon of a case conference. The patients begin to learn of the referents of their thoughts, now newly described in a syntax of wishes and interactions with direct and indirect objects of those wishes. These new formulations in sentences should fit into statements about actual current interactions with people and assimilated into the template of past experiences as well as describe the relationship to the analyst. Thus, a three-way demand is made. The descriptions in words ought to fit past, present, and transference by just changing tense, person, and object of the verb.

While stressing the universality of the form of the intervention, I would like to suggest that, even if recent linguists have looked for universals, they also are curious about how specific linguistic events are related to those universals. This concern is naturally more evident in those who pursue performance variables rather than competence. Chomsky (1978), in a recent paper on language and unconscious knowledge, quotes Freud as saying that a dream is nothing more than a particular form of thinking. Earlier in that same essay, Chomsky states "for the scientist interested in the nature of language it is the general principles that are finally important. The special properties of particular languages are of much less interest. For the normal person dealing with language in his daily life, precisely the opposite is true" (p. 24). And indeed, for the psychotherapist, the latter is the preferred position if the clinical problem is the specific concern. Still, we cannot function as though each sentence were unique and unrelated to some more generally available grammar.

The task of the psychotherapy is and must be dually directed. We take for granted that our patient's language is related to the language of others, just as we take for granted the Oedipus complex as a universal nuclear complex. However, the therapist's task is different from that of the contextless grammarian insofar as he directs his attention toward breaking into the personal idiom of the patient, penetrating his or her style and general linguistic form and then judging what kind of verbal intervention will make a difference. Structurally, we have found the referent for style to be a complex organization of genetic factors bound by defense and wish deriving from the past and sequentially reformed to be repeated in the present. These latter features are as much an appeal to universals as is Chomsky's, but in terms of the likely event of all individuals developing autonomy from dependency in a world of two-sexed persons.

The interpretation of these forms and their breakdown into analyzed moieties loosens fixed links which the patient treats as though they were obligatory. The aim of therapy, if you will, is to increase the flexibility of possible patient responsiveness via the interpretation of the meaning of the ideas and behaviors that emerge in his life and experiences. Each new interpretation of events held so rigidly by the patient permits the judgment that former categories no longer apply and are more appropriate to the past. Such significance, as formerly held, derives from a vision of reality which is full of the animism of early life. On the other hand, if one dwelled only on the past, one would have a science of early history—indeed, a revisionist's history. Rather, the past is dwelled on because it helps people realize the genetic continuity with that past and the ever present impact of that past on the present.

Let me explain the idea that a neurosis or neurotic character structure may be looked at as the behavioral outcome of adherence to a rigid set of symbols. Everything in the experience of a neurotic is looked at as a representative icon which results in inflexibility of action. For example, phobic displacements occur because of a misapprehension which is useful, because the patient can adaptively avoid that which he thinks of as dangerous. To help undo the rigid system described, dynamic psychotherapy elaborates the determinants of how the phobic object stands for something other than itself. The avoidance becomes rational, and the patient feels understood when he understands the phobic object as a psychoanalytic symbol. The obsessional patient must also rethink his conscious thoughts and come to realize that they represent persistence of deep structrual content which Freud subsumed under the notion of *pressure of the drives*. The obsessional's conscious thoughts in words also stand for something which he does not fully recognize. The obsessions limit activities—they fill the patient with doubt and create a stylistic pattern that necessitates repeated doing and undoing that ends in fruitless, aimless work, except that the activity keeps anxiety at a lower pitch.

When looked at from the standpoint of the psychoanalytic symbol, we must search for an unconscious referent in both obsessional and phobic activities. When looked at from the standpoint of linguistic symbols, we can recognize in each instance that there is an apparent lack of referent linking the observed symptom to the unconscious. Indeed, the phobic object and obsessions seem meaningless and are apparently arbitrary. That arbitrariness derives from the denotative aspect of the symptoms not being related by the usual linguistic conventions. The code is obscure. Rather they are related to the deeper referent as a sign, that is, the iconic representations have to be discovered within the individual's idiosyncratic lexicon derived from schemata built during development. Therapy with neurotics involves the careful establishment of the links in their personal etymologic history by which they derive their rigid symptom forms. These must be redefined and unleashed from their past determinants. The model can be carried further to impulsive individuals who relate to their world with almost sensory-motor immediacy. They function as though the sign were a signal. Clearly, all three elements of the referential system ought to be available in a flexibly functioning individual who may boast a relative degree of health. As noted in Chapter 6, differing circumstances of life require different kinds of symbolic responsiveness, but assumed maturity should permit selective application toward all signs in an adaptive shift from their signal sign and symbol implications.

Psychoses present another problem. As previously mentioned, Freud viewed the psychotic process as one in which the individual suffering a psychosis has lost the connection between word and thing presentations. Instead, words were treated as though they were things, and the joy in manipulating the words in a concrete manner creates a confusion in the listener as to what it is that is being described. Werner and Kaplan (1963) suggested that the basic problem in schizophrenic language is that referential spheres are suffused with higly personal themes. Moreover, the themes lack natural contour, and there is "leakage" from one sphere to another. Common words are used more idiosyncratically than in neurotics, and affective and conative imperatives spill over into the discourse of the psychotic.

Although no syntactic problems have been found in the nonthought-disordered psychotic (except in those rare instances of word salad), characteristic problems in coding of language have been pinpointed via linguistic methods in thought-disordered schizophrenics when they are segregated from nonthought-disordered schizophrenics. Rochester's (1977) group from Toronto suggested that the listener operates under a "processing overload" when trying to understand the schizophrenic with a thought disorder. They demonstrated this effect by first asking clinicians to distinguish thought-disordered from nonthought-disordered subjects. Transcripts of the speech of each group were provided for lay judges, who were asked to mark sets of phrases for coherence and ability to be understood. The researchers found that blind lay judges had an impressive 75% hit rate and only a 0 to 5% false-alarm rate in distinguishing the thought-disordered subjects from nonthought-disordered subjects. Six linguistic variables were then used to check what distinguished one group from the other. A 60% hit rate and a 10 to 15% false-alarm rate resulted from this approach. The authors were able to identify the bases on which the lay judges made these distinctions and found that linguistic variables could predict about 38% of the judges' evaluations. Rochester and her colleagues suggested that had they included intonational marking and the structure by which verbs presuppose referent information, they might have brought their predictive variables up to a much higher figure, but they did not carry out these operations. Two problems emerged as central from their data: a thought-disordered speaker seems to alert his listener to search for information which is not forthcoming. Moreover, that same psychotic speaker ties clauses together with lexical bonds, using tangential associations to the words. Psychotic subjects rarely use an extensive set of conjunctive bonds—this also leaves it up to the listener to provide cohesive bonding between clauses. One has an impression similar to that of listening to poetry—or rather the problem of listening to difficult poetry. Forrest (1965) made a similar analogy of the language of schizophrenia to the formation of poetry. Rochester's group noted that Cameron's (1944) asyndetic thinking represented a parallel concept.

All the features outlined indicate that the psychotic speaker is more likely to use additive conjunctions such as *and* to string clauses together rather than the more useful conjunctions *but, so; then,* and *well.* On the other hand, their lexical associations may be highly personal as mentioned. When doing therapy with the psychotic patient, the auditor has a tendency to feel that he has been left out, because of the highly idiosyncratic referential system employed. This circumstance dictates one of the features of listening to the psychotic. The therapist must accommodate himself by inducing a relative suspension of listening within the rules of secondary process. He must find other ways to grasp how the psychotic uses words from the gestalt of the discourse and all the paralinguistic cues at his disposal. Indeed, it is probable that each psychotic has his own stylistic variables which must be listened for in order to be "in on" his thoughts—or at least "in on" his singular linguistic links before the therapist can understand the thought processes that the linguistic forms connote. Great variability in shifting reference also has to be accommodated.

If one can engage the psychotic individual into the cooperative effort and make him understand that there is a party listening who would like to understand what is said, it will be possible to use that cooperation to breach the barrier that is set up by the egocentric use of the code. To be sure, this personalized use of the code is the very fact that has given rise to the idea that the intention of the psychotic is to isolate himself. The surmise of dynamic therapists is that he does so because of his inability to regulate the interpersonal sphere rather than because of a linguistic-cognitive barrier. The fact may be that the truth lies between these alternatives. Part of the defensiveness of that isolation might be reflected in the linguistic barrier. Some therapists use the technique with psychotics of confronting them with their "crazy talk"; admonishing them to adopt, if they can, a more standard code to forward a therapeutic contract.

When the listener has more leeway in time and pressure, he may be content to accept the psychotic's delivery; he may listen as though listening to poetic discourse and thereafter risk interpretative remarks to suggest to the psychotic that he has understood the poetry. I do not mean to say that the barrier to understanding psychotic language is the same as the barrier to understanding poetry, but rather that similar linguistic pitfalls or mechanisms may be pertinent. In this sense, Freud's comment that the dream is like the language of the psychotic and that primary process is more relatively abundant in psychotic speech makes some sense—both may draw on the tools that enable an analysis of the rebus.

Moving along to psychotherapy with the borderline patient, one would think his or her speech and language organization would cohere with the variables that have been invoked to make that diagnosis in the first place. Borderline patients are individuals who tend toward impulsiveness, present problems of esteem regulation, diffusion of identity, body-image instability, and the use of primitive ego defenses. Nonetheless, reality testing is maintained, for the most part, with a fluid difficulty in reality sense. The use of body language is most evident in the hypochondriacal concerns of many borderlines, and hystericallike transformations are common (see Kernberg, 1978; Masterson, 1978; Searles, 1975). A formal analysis of the linguistic style of borderline patients may reveal their difficulties in object relations. The paralinguistics as well as the linguistic style that they adopt is often telling, especially in individuals who have a tendency toward "as if" transient structures. Their language use may reveal the characteristics of assuming the magic impact of words. They believe in the illocutionary force of what is said as an effector of change. This expectation is often thwarted by the patient himself when the obverse side of his splitting transference is revealed. The therapist may at any one point in the therapeutic process find that he is addressed as either part of the split object.

Again, the syntactic structure of the borderline patient would tend to be no different from that of the average neurotic, and the structural components to be noted should be observed within the performance of the speech act, revealing the belief in relative nonseparation of minds and the symbiotic immediacy of the transmission of ideas, without the patient fully grasping the depth of the communicative barrier.

The therapeutic intent in treating the borderline patient remains the same, in that the therapist continues to interpet the meaning of the patient's behavior and statements. In turn, the borderline patient may enjoin the therapist into other human interactions than speech; he comes to therapy with preconceived ideas about its conduct just as the neurotic's unconscious aim may diverge from his conscious wish for cure. The borderline patient may enjoy the game of talking for its relational satisfaction and have very little intention to understand or communicate. Some of these individuals may be of high intelligence, but their intellectual capacities are split-off, permitting sequestered pockets of ideas which do not partake of fully rational mechanisms. The tendency to split may make of the therapist only one part of a love/hate or idealized/demeaned dichotomy. Technically, nowhere is it more important than with the borderline patient to stage one's interpretation, initially bringing the attention of the patient to his tendency to act and use his speech as an action substitute. The therapist may then point to the patient's tendency to categorize along conceptual dimensions of "all or none" affective components, such as completely hated or completely loved categories. However, the excessive sensitivity of the borderline patient demands that one not offend him by the continuing feeling that he is being criticized. This poses a difficult problem in the therapy of such individuals, because wording has to be cast in such a way that the indicative aspect of what is being said is prominent, rather than the critical aspects which would lead ultimately to change.

Some therapists employ other media than words. Straker, (1978) in an unpublished set of case studies, indicated the use of diagrams which he and the patient can point to as a practical means of showing the degree to which the borderline individual believes himself to be a part of the object under certain stressful conditions leading to regression. He therefore might find it unnecessary to communicate clearly. In turn, the borderline patient's wish for immediate closeness yields anxiety. His destructive tendencies toward the object, in the absence of the therapist, make it very important to think of what might be called the *amulet function* of the therapist (see Greenacre, 1960, 1969). How can the patient take away from the therapeutic hour the sense that the therapist is continually available in an amulet fashion even when not in sight? The notion of the incantation function of words may be useful here (see Cassirer, 1946). The hoped for continuing memory of the therapist, stored within the patient as the words-of-the-therapist, is facilitative to the treatment alliance with the borderline. Just as children say their new words in bed in the manner that transitional objects are fondled, the therapist's presence may be recreated for such patients by offering them easy-to-remember almost epigrammatic phrases. Some therapists find it important to repeat interpretations in the same form to guarantee storage. The ultimate move in borderline patients toward decentering them from subject–object fusion toward the possibility of empathy with others can only be achieved when the psychological object corresponds more closely to the person of the therapist. The reference to the inner object should ultimately correspond to a referent that is a sustaining inner image that can be both loved and hated and not split in accord with prior primitivized categories. The ability to predicate and tolerate a kind of grammatical ambivalence is a central therapeutic aim for such individuals.

If therapists, because of their prior theoretical stance, handle words in a way that is concretely related to mechanistic images of causal chains, it will further ensconce misapprehensions in patients. There is a tendency among many therapists to use locutions which mislead and which are used as inexact interpretations by patients. Schafer (1976, 1978a,b) has alerted us to a number of locutions which have arisen within our therapeutic vocabulary. For example, the phrase "getting one's feelings out" leads to the idea of a storage area for feelings and the idea of feelings as a volume-filling substance. An anal model of retention that leads to poisoning is conjured up. On the other hand, expressing the feelings becomes "good." The latter stance may not always be salutary, especially in fragile individuals to whom the expression of violent emotions becomes very frightening and even threatening to core ego organizations. Such expressions also foster the erroneous idea that to verbalize one's feelings is, in itself, therapeutic, rather than making such verbalization a *means* toward understanding, which can then be used therapeutically. Even Freud's metaphor of the foreign body in hysteria was a notion that it is the foreign body that continues the suppuration—the generation of bad feelings. It was not the feelings that had to be gotten out but the *idea* which generated the feelings. The idea can only be subjected to corrective interpretation when verbalized and shared.

Another frequent locution centers about the patient's tendency to talk about his moods and feelings as though they were "visited upon him" and that he is a passive victim of these somewhat alien intruders. We are all aware of the mode of description in classical literature in

which the gods induce varying dilemmas and create emotions and mishap in the lives of Homeric characters. Such a vision of man permits
one's own ideas not to be the source of emotional constellations. Such
phrases as "my depression makes me do this" or "my sadness weighs
me down" are paraphrases of the victimization of the patient by the
mood. Oral concretization is heard frequently, too: The patient expects
to "take in" something from the therapist. An audition becomes an
enunciation with the expectation of a subsequent pregnancy that will
result in a kind of messianic birth which constitutes a cure. Passivity is
expressed in such therapies, with the patient listening to the wisdom of
the therapist with the expectation of emerging whole and cured. That
attitude is a misapprehension that comes from the overapplication of
oral-aural intercourse. It is difficult for many patients to get the idea very
early in therapy that they have to do things about their lives as a result of
the understanding brought about by the therapeutic discourse, and that
the cure does not come as a passive result of being talked to.

In a similar fashion, many patients talk about anger as a noun,
rather than angry ideas and angry actions. One of the gravest difficulties
that has evolved from Freud's dual instinct theory comes from the concretization of the theory of drives in therapeutic language. If one's aggression and one's libido are made manifest in ways that one is not
accustomed to call angry or libidinous, then it would be very hard for the
patient to understand how his actions and behaviors might be called
aggressive or sexual derivatives. The passive-aggressive individual, for
example, does not readily see how his inactivity or his quietness may be
an angry act until he can understand that such behaviors are unique
ways of rendering an unconscious angry thought complex. Again, the
reference is vague until its meaning is available to consciousness. The
seductive woman or man may not understand that it is not sexuality (a
noun) being expressed, but rather that her or his behavior is interpreted
by others as sexual. The frequent cry of "Who me?" reveals the sexually
preoccupied patient's lack of understanding that it is *in* his or her *behavior* that these notions are made manifest or classified as such and not
in the consciousness of the intent as an idea.

As noted in Chapter 9, therapists who say "You think such and
such" miss the boat because the patient very readily might answer "I
have never thought that." If one were to reply "But that's what we mean
by unconscious," it still would not serve as an explanation unless the
individual can be shown by his or her own experience. We must show
patients that what they say and do become indicative of ideas which are

not expressed in the usual manner. The reference–referent congruence is as much at stake here as in any semiotic system.

One of the most difficult areas to approach in language concerns the designation of conflict. Many therapists resort to linguistic forms which denote fragmenting the self. They present conflicts as battles between parts of the self—rather than the "you" and the environment to which the individual is expected to adapt. It is very difficult to point to the warring features within, without temporarily upsetting the cohesion of the self (see Grossman & Simon, 1969). The dream becomes an important linguistic vehicle for expressing the buried agencies within and a convenient example of conflict representation. Although the dream may represent aspects of conflict in images of individuals from one's life or imagination as though they were separate from the self, each image must ultimately be translated into the waking thought and looked at as features or aspects of one's own thought and feeling states. Like figures in a morality play, dream images and dream figures concretize thoughts. The discovery of the syntax of the dream and the tendencies of the dreamer to organize his or her sleeping thoughts in a certain manner is a very useful instrument, which, once designated, can be pointed to and repointed to and used to bring home an appropriate interpretation of conflict.

Having mentioned the dream, I would like to highlight the tendency of the patient to use the dream as an object of his interest rather than as a mode of mentation continuous with waking thoughts. Disowning or discounting the dream because it seems illogical or occurs during sleep renders the patient relatively helpless, because the dream seems to impinge upon his senses, upon his memory without willing it, permitting disavowel as unwished. Since not all dreams are analyzed fully, it is difficult for the patient to appreciate the significance of the dream as communication unless he has some experience of success in understanding his dreams at some time in the therapy. The more success that one has at interpretation of dreams determines the breadth of the understanding possible in the future use of dreams as a basis for thinking about one's thoughts.

The final refuge of many patients, regardless of diagnosis, involves the inexpressible. The inexpressible is the final refuge of the one-mind world—*solipsism*. Encouraging a patient to say in words that which he thought could not be put into words is the aim of talking therapies. It is only with this activity that potentials for insight and cure are possible. We cannot accept the excuse of the inexpressible, because the inexpressible then prescribes the limits of our therapy and is often used defensively. It is the therapist's job, in turn, to tolerate the broadest variety of expressions and ultimately use the vehicle of words in sentences as the most parsimonious means available for rendering feelings and ideas into a communicated something. If the ultimate aim of the therapy is to build a coherent story for a patient so that he may move in his life with greater freedom and flexibility, then he has to have his actions, thoughts, and feelings condensed and clearly designated. There is no better human way to do this than through language. Whatever is done that is therapeutic derives from rendering reasonable and rational that which had plagued patients as though mysterious and irrational. Putting those ideas into words makes change possible. Linguistics, psycholinguistics, and their relation to the study of our ways of knowing provide a broader framework for psychotherapists to use for their better understanding of what patients say—and also for better understanding of the formal underpinnings of what therapists say to patients.

References

Abraham, K. A. A short study of the development of the libido. In *Selected Papers on Psychoanalysis*. New York: Basic Books, 1953. (Originally published, 1924.)

Allport, F. H. *Theories of perception and the concept of structures*. New York: Wiley, 1955.

Andreasen, N. J. C., & Pfohl, B. Linguistic analysis of speech in affective disorders. *Archives of General Psychiatry*, 1976, *33*, 1361–1367.

Anthony, E. J. Between yes and no. *Journal of Psychosocial Process: Issues in Child Mental Health*, 1974, *3*, 23–46.

Aries, P. *Centuries of childhood: A social history of family life*. New York: Knopf, 1962.

Austin, J. L. *How to do things with words*. New York: Oxford University Press, 1962.

Balkanyi, C. On verbalization. *International Journal of Psychoanalysis*, 1964, *45*, 64–74.

Bates, E. *Language and context: The acquisition of pragmatics*. New York: Academic Press, 1976.

Bateson, G., & Jackson, D. D. Social factors and disorders of communication: Some varieties of pathogenic organization. *Research Publications, Association for Research in Nervous and Mental Disease*, 1964, *42*, 270–290.

Bateson, G., Jackson, D. D., Haley, J., & Weakland, J. Toward a theory of schizophrenia. *Behavioral Science*, 1956, *1*, 251–264.

Beres, D. The unconscious fantasy. *Psychoanalytic Quarterly*, 1962, *31*, 309–328.

Bloom, L. *Language development: Form and function in emerging grammars*. Cambridge: M.I.T. Press, 1970.

Bloomfield, L. *Language*. New York: Holt, 1933.

Bowlby, J. The nature of the child's tie to his mother. *International Journal of Psychoanalysis*, 1958, *39*, 350–373.

Breslow, R. E. *Communication. Auditory feedback and motor behavior*. Unpublished manuscript, 1979.

Bronowski, J., & Bellugi, U. Language, name and concept. *Science*, 1970, *168*, 669–673.

Brown, R. *A first language: The early stages*. Cambridge: Harvard University Press, 1973.

Brown, R. W. *Words and things*. New York: Free Press, 1958.

Brown, R. W., & Bellugi, V. Three processes in the child's acquisition of syntax. In E. Lenneberg (Ed.), *New directions in the study of language*. Cambridge: M.I.T. Press, 1964.

Bruner, J. S. The ontogenesis of speech acts. *Journal of Child Language*, 1974, *2*, 1–19.

Bühler, K. *Sprachtheorie*. Jena: Fischer Verlag, 1934.

Cameron, N. Experimental analysis of schizophrenic thinking. In J. S. Kasanin (Ed.), *Language and thought in schizophrenia*. Berkeley: University of California Press, 1944.

Carroll, L. *The annotated Alice: Alice's adventures in wonderland and through the looking glass*. New York: Clarkson N. Potter, 1970.

Cassirer, E. *Language and myth. New York: Dover, 1946.*

Cassirer, E. *An essay on man.* New York: Doubleday, 1953.

Chafe, W. L. *Meaning and the structure of langauge.* Chicago: University of Chicago Press, 1970.

Cherry, C. *On human communication.* Cambridge: M.I.T. Press, 1957.

Chisholm, R. M. The contrary-to-fact conditional. In H. Feigl & W. Sellars (Eds.), *Readings in philosophical analysis.* New York: Appleton-Century-Crofts, 1949.

Chomsky, N. *Syntactic structures.* The Hague: Mouton, 1957.

Chomsky, N. *Aspects of the theory of syntax.* Cambridge: M.I.T. Press, 1965.

Chomsky, N. *Reflections on language.* New York: Pantheon Books, 1975.

Chomsky, N. Language and unconscious knowledge. In J. H. Smith (Ed.), *Psychoanalysis and language* (Vol. 3). New Haven: Yale University Press, 1978.

Condon, W. S., & Sander, L. Neonate movement is synchronized with adult speech. *Science,* 1974, *183,* 99–101.

Cummings, E. E. *Collected Poems.* New York: Harcourt Brace, 1926.

Dahl, H., Teller, V., Moss, D., & Trujillo, M. Countertransference examples of the syntactic expression of worded-off contents. *Psychoanalytic Quarterly,* 1978, *47,* 339–363.

Darwin, C. *The origin of the species.* London: Watts, 1929.

Doolittle, H. *Tribute to Freud.* New York: Pantheon Books, 1956.

Edelheit, H. Speech and psychic structures. *Journal of the American Psychoanalytic Association,* 1969, *17,* 381–412.

Edelheit, H. Mythopoiesis and the primal scene. In W. Muensterberger & A. H. Esman (Eds.), *The Psychoanalytic study of society* (Vol. 5). New York: International Universities Press, 1972.

Edelheit, H. On the biology of language: Darwinian/Larmarckian homology in human inheritance (with some thoughts about the Larmarckism of Freud). In J. H. Smith (Ed.), *Psychoanalysis and language.* New Haven: Yale University Press, 1978.

Edelson, M. Language and dreams: The interpretation of dreams revisited. In R. Eissler (Ed.), *The psychoanalytic study of the child* (Vol. 27). New York: Quadrangle Books, 1972.

Edelson, M. *Language and interpretation in psychoanalysis.* New Haven: Yale University Press, 1975.

Edelson, M. Toward a study of interpretation in psychoanalysis. In J. J. Loubster *et al.* (Eds.), *Explorations in general theory in social science* (Vol. 1). New York: Free Press, 1976.

Eliot, T. S. *The lovesong of J. Alfred Prufrock.* New York: Harcourt Brace, 1930.

Eliot, T. S. *Collected Poems.* New York: Harcourt Brace, 1930.

Emde, R. N., Gaensbauer, T. J., & Harmon, R. J. *Emotional expression in infancy: A biobehavioral study.* New York: International Universities Press, 1976.

Erikson, E. H. *Identity: Youth and crisis.* New York: W. W. Norton, 1968.

Feldman, S. S. *Mannerisms of speech and gestures in everyday life.* New York: International Universities Press, 1959.

Fenichel, O. *Problems of psychoanalysis technique.* New York: The Psychoanalytic Quarterly Press, 1941.

Forrest, D. W. Poiesis and the language of schizophrenia. *Psychiatry, Journal for the Study of Interpersonal Processes,* 1965, *28,* 1–18.

Fouts, R. S. Acquisition and testing of gestural signs in four young chimpanzees. *Science,* 1973, *180,* 978–980.

Freedman, N. Hands, words, and mind: On the structuralization of body movements during discourse and the capacity for verbal representation. *Communicative Structures and Psychic Structures,* 1977, *1,* 109–132.

Freedman, N., & Steingart, I. Kinesic internalization and language construction. In D. P. Spence (Ed.), *Psychoanalysis and contemporary science* (Vol. 4). New York: International Universities Press, 1975.

Frege, G. On sense and nominatum. In H. Feigl & W. Sellars (Eds.), *Readings in philosophical analysis*. New York: Appleton-Century-Crofts, 1949.

Freud, S. (1891) *On aphasia*. (E. Stengel, trans.) New York: International Universities Press, 1953.

Freud, S. *Studies on hysteria*. In *Complete Works* (Vol. 2), Standard Edition. London: Hogarth Press, 1955. (Originally published 1893–1895.)

Freud, S. *Project for a scientific psychology*. In *Complete Works* (Vol. 1), Standard Edition. London: Hogarth Press, 1953. (Originally published, 1895.)

Freud, S. *The interpretation of dreams*. In *Complete Works* (Vols. 4 and 5), Standard Edition. London: Hogarth Press, 1953. (Originally published, 1900.)

Freud, S. *The psychopathology of everyday life*. In *Complete Works* (Vol. 6), Standard Edition. London: Hogarth Press, 1960. (Originally published, 1901.)

Freud, S. *Obsessive actions and religious practices*. In *Complete Works* (Vol. 9), Standard Edition. London: Hogarth Press, 1959. (Originally published, 1907.)

Freud, S. *The antithetical meaning of primal words*. In *Complete Works* (Vol. 11), Standard Edition. London: Hogarth Press, 1957. (Originally published, 1910.)

Freud, S. *Psychoanalytic notes on an autobiographical account of a case of paranoia*. In *Complete Works* (Vol. 12), Standard Edition. London: Hogarth Press, 1958. (Originally published, 1911.)

Freud, S. *Recommendations to physicians practising psychoanalysis*. In *Complete Works* (Vol. 12), Standard Edition. London: Hogarth Press, 1958. (Originally published, 1912–1914.)

Freud, S. *The philological interest of psychoanalysis*. In *Complete Works* (Vol. 13), Standard Edition. London: Hogarth Press, 1955. (Originally published, 1913.)

Freud, S. *The unconscious*. In *Complete Works* (Vol. 14), Standard Edition. London: Hogarth Press, 1957. (Originally published, 1915.)

Freud, S. *Introductory lectures on psychoanalysis I and II*. In *Complete Works* (Vol. 15), Standard Edition. London: Hogarth Press, 1963. (Originally published, 1915–1916.)

Freud, S. *From the history of an infantile neurosis*. In *Complete Works* (Vol. 17), Standard Edition. London: Hogarth Press, 1955. (Originally published, 1918.)

Freud, S. *Neurosis and psychosis*. In *Complete Works* (Vol. 19), Standard Edition. London: Hogarth Press, 1961. (a) (Originally published, 1924).

Freud, S. *Loss of reality in neurosis and psychosis*. In *Complete Works* (Vol. 19), Standard Edition. London: Hogarth Press, 1961. (b) (Originally published, 1924.)

Freud, S. *Negation*. In *Complete Works* (Vol. 19), Standard Edition. London: Hogarth Press, 1961. (c) (Originally published, 1925.)

Freud, S. *An outline of psychoanalysis*. In *Complete Works* (Vol. 23), Standard Edition. London: Hogarth Press, 1964. (Originally published, 1940.)

Fries, M. E., Woolf, P. J. Some hypotheses on the role of congenital activity type in personality development. *The Psychoanalytic Study of the Child*, 1953, *8*, 48–62.

Fromm-Reichmann, F., & Halle, M. *Recent advances in psychoanalytic therapy*. New York: Hermitage Press, 1949.

Frosch, J. Transference derivatives of the family romance. *Journal of the American Psychoanalytic Association*, 1959, *7*, 503–522.

Gallie, W. B. *Peirce and pragmatism*. Middlesex, England: Pelican Books, 1952.

Gardner, R. A., & Gardner, B. T. Teaching sign language to a chimpanzee. *Science*, 1969, *165*, 664–672.

Gardner, R. A., & Gardner, B. T. Early signs of language in child and chimpanzee. *Science*, 1975, *187*, 752–753.

Glover, E. *The technique of psychoanalysis*. New York: International Universities Press, 1955.

Grand, S. On hand movements during speech: Studies of the role of self-stimulation in communication under conditions of psychopathology, sensory deficit, and bilingualism. *Communicative Structures and Psychic Structures*, 1977, *1*, 199–221.

Grand, S., Breslow, R., & Freedman, N. *On the role of reduced auditory feedback and kinesic self-stimulation during Stroop Color-Word Performance.* Unpublished manuscript, 1978.

Greenacre, P. Further notes on fetishism. *The Psychoanalytic Study of the Child*, 1960, *15*, 191–207.

Greenacre, P. The fetish and the transitional object. *The Psychoanalytic Study of the Child*, 1969, *24*, 144–164.

Grossman, W. I., & Simon, B. Anthropomorphism: Motive, meaning, and causality in psychoanalytic theory. *The Psychoanalytic Study of the Child*, 1969, *24*, 78–114.

Grossman, W. I., & Stewart, W. A. Penis envy: From childhood wish to developmental metaphor. *Journal of the American Psychoanalytic Association*, 1976, *24*, 193–212.

Haeckel, E. *The evolution of man* (Vol. 1). New York: D. Appleton, 1879.

Halliday, M. A. K. *Learning how to mean: Explorations in the development of language.* London: Edward Arnold, 1975.

Harlow, H. F., Plubell, P. E., & Baysinger, C. M. Induction of psychological death in Rhesus monkeys. *Journal of Autism and Childhood Schizophrenia*, 1973, *3*, 299–307.

Harner, L. Children's understanding of linguistic reference to past and future. *Journal of Psycholinguistic Research*, 1976, *5*, 65–84.

Hartmann, H. Technical implications of ego psychology. *Psychoanalytic Quarterly*, 1951, *20*, 31–43.

Hartmann, H. The mutual influences in the development of ego and id. *The Psychoanalytic Study of the Child*, 1952, *7*, 9–30.

Hartmann, H. *Ego psychology and the problem of adaptation.* New York: International Universities Press, 1958. (Originally published, 1939.)

Healy, A. F. Can chimpanzees learn a phonemic language? *Journal of Psycholinguistic Research*, 1973, *2*, 167–170.

Heffner, E. *Mothering.* New York: Doubleday, 1978.

Hockett, C. D. The origin of speech. *The Scientific American*, 1960, *203*, 88–96.

Jacobs, T. Posture, gesture and movement in the analyst: Cues to interpretation and countertransference. *Journal of the American Psychoanalytic Association*, 1973, *21*, 71–92.

Jakobovits, L., & Lambert, W. Semantic satiation among bilinguals. *Journal of Experimental Psychology*, 1961, *67*, 567–582.

Jakobson, R., & Halle, M. *Fundamentals of language.* The Hague: Mouton, 1956.

Jakobson, R., Fant, C., & Halle, M. *Preliminaries to speech analysis.* Cambridge: M.I.T. Press, 1969.

Jespersen, O. *Language, its nature, development and origin.* New York: W. W. Norton, 1964.

Johnson, A. Sanctions for super ego lacunae of adolescents. In K. Eissler (Ed.), *Searchlights on delinquency.* New York: International Universities Press, 1949.

Kaden, S. E., Wapher, S., & Werner, H. Studies in physiognomic perception: II. Effect of directional dynamics of pictured objects and of words on the position of the apparent horizon. *Journal of Psychology*, 1955, *39*, 61–70.

Katan, A. Some thoughts about the role of verbalization in early childhood. *The Psychoanalytic Study of the Child*, 1961, *16*, 184–188.

Katz, J. J., & Bever, T. G. The fall and rise of empiricism. In T. Bever & D. T. Langendoen (Eds.), *An integrated theory of linguistic ability.* New York: T. Y. Crowell, 1976.

Kaufman, I. C. The waning of the mother-infant bond in two species of Macaque. In B. M. Foss (Ed.), *Determinants of infant behavior* (Vol. 4). London: Methuen, 1969.

Kaufman, I. C., & Rosenblum, L. A. A behavioral taxonomy for Macaca nemestrina and Macaca radiata: Based on longitudinal observations of family groups in the lab. *Primates*, 1966, *7*, 205–258.

Kellogg, W. N. Communication and language in the home-raised chimpanzee. *Science,* 1968, *162,* 423–427.

Kernberg, O. F. Structural change and its impediments. In P. Hartocollis (Ed.), *Borderline personality disorders: The concept, the syndrome, the patient.* New York: International Universities Press, 1977. (a)

Kernberg, O. F. Structural diagnosis of borderline personality organizations. In P. Hartocollis (Ed.), *Borderline personality disorders: The concept, the syndrome, the patient.* New York: International Universities Press, 1977.(b)

Kernberg, O. F. Contrasting approaches to the psychotherapy of borderline conditions. In J. Masterson (Ed.), *New perspectives on psychotherapy of the borderline adult.* New York: Brunner/Mazel, 1978.

Kestenberg, J. Development of the young child as expressed through bodily movement. *Journal of the American Psychoanalytic Association,* 1971, *74,* 1–22.

Klaus, M. H., & Kennel, J. H. *Maternal-infant bonding.* St. Louis: C. V. Mosby, 1976.

Kohut, H. *The restoration of the self.* New York: International Universities Press, 1977.

Koos, E. L. *The health of Regionville.* New York: Columbia University Press, 1954.

Kris, E. On inspiration. *International Journal of Psychoanalysis,* 1939, *20,* 377–389.

Kris, E. On preconscious mental processes. *Psychoanalytic Quarterly,* 1950, *19,* 540–560.

Kris, E. On some vicissitudes of insight in psychoanalysis. *International Journal of Psychoanalysis,* 1956, *37,* 1–11.

Labov, W., & Fanshel, D. *Therapeutic discourse.* New York: Academic Press, 1977.

Lacan, J. *The language of the self: The function of language in psychoanalysis.* (Translated by A. Wilden). Baltimore: The Johns Hopkins Press, 1956.

Lakoff, G. On generative semantics. In D. D. Steinberg & L. A. Jakobovits (Eds.), *Semantics.* London: Cambridge University Press, 1971.

Langer, S. K. *Mind: An essay on human feeling* (Vol. 1). Baltimore: The Johns Hopkins Press, 1967.

Lashley, K. S. The problem of serial order in behavior. In L. A. Jeffress (Ed.), *Cerebral mechanisms in behavior: The Hixon symposium.* New York: Wiley, 1951.

Lenneberg, E. H. *Biological foundation of language.* New York: Wiley, 1967.

Lenneberg, E. H., & Lenneberg, E. *Foundations of language development: A multidisciplinary approach* (Vols. 1 and 2). New York: Academic Press, 1975.

Leopold, W. F. *Speech development in a bilingual child.* Evanston: Northwestern University Press, 1939–1949.

Lewin, B. D. Some observations on knowledge, belief, and the impulse to know. *International Journal of Psychoanalysis,* 1939, *20,* 426–431.

Lewin, B. D. *The psychoanalysis of elation.* New York: W. W. Norton, 1950.

Lewis, C. I. Some logical considerations concerning the mental. In H. Feigl & W. Sellars (Eds.), *Readings in philosophical analysis.* New York: Appleton-Century-Crofts, 1949.

Lewis, M. M. *Infant speech.* New York: Harcourt Brace, 1936.

Lewis, M. M. *How children learn to speak.* New York: Basic Books, 1959.

Loewald, H. W. Psychoanalytic theory and the psychoanalytic process. *The Psychoanalytic Study of the Child,* 1970, *25,* 45–68.

Loewenstein, R. M. The problem of interpretation. *Psychoanalytic Quarterly,* 1951, *20,* 1–14.

Loewenstein, R. M. Some remarks on the role of speech in psychoanalytic technique. *International Journal of Psychoanalysis,* 1956, *37,* 460–468.

Luria, A. R. *The role of speech in the regulation of normal and abnormal behavior.* New York: Liveright Public Corporation, 1961.

McCawley, J. D. The role of semantics in grammar. In E. Bach & R. T. Harms (Eds.), *Universals in linguistic theory.* New York: Holt, 1968.

McNeill, D., & McNeill, N. B. A question in semantic development: What does a child mean when he says "No?" Paper presented to the Society for Research in Child Development, 1967.

McQuown, N. E., Bateson, G., Birdwhistell, R., Brosen, H., & Hockett, C. The natural history of an interview. *Microfilm Collection of Manuscripts in Cultural Anthropology.* Chicago: University of Chicago Library, 1971.

Maher, B. The languages of schizophrenics: A review and interpretation. *British Journal of Psychiatry*, 1972, *120*, 3–17.

Mahler, M. S., Pine, F., & Bergman, A. *The psychological birth of the human infant.* New York: Basic Books, 1975.

Major, R. *Rêver l'autre: La psychanalyse prise au mot.* Paris: Aubier-Montaigne, 1977.

Masterson, J. *New perspectives on psychotherapy of the borderline adult.* New York: Brunner/ Mazel, 1978.

Mead, G. H. *Mind, self and society.* Chicago: University of Chicago Press, 1934.

Mead, G. H. *The social psychology of C. H. Mead.* Chicago: University of Chicago Press, 1956.

Menninger, K. A. *Theory of psychoanalytic technique.* New York: Basic Books, 1958.

Meyer, A. *Psychobiology: A science of man.* Springfield, Ill.: Charles C Thomas, 1957.

Miller, G. A. Language and psychology. In E. H. Lenneberg (Ed.), *New directions in the study of language.* Cambridge: M.I.T. Press, 1964.

Miller, G. A. *Spontaneous apprentices: Children and language.* New York: Seabury Press, 1977.

Miller, G. A. *Images and models, similes and metaphors.* Unpublished manuscript, 1979.

Milne, A. A. *When we were very young.* New York: E. P. Dutton, 1961. (a)

Milne, A. A. *Now we are six.* New York: E. P. Dutton, 1961. (b)

Morris, C. *Signification and significance: A study of the relations of signs and values.* Cambridge: M.I.T. Press, 1964.

Needles, W. Gesticulation and speech. *International Journal of Psychoanalysis*, 1959, *40*, 291–294.

Ninio, A., Bruner, J. The achievement and antecedents of labelling. *Journal of Child Language*, 1978, *5*, 1–15.

Nunberg, H. The will to recovery. In his *Practice and Theory of Psychoanalysis* (Vol. 1). New York: International Universities Press, 1948. (Originally published, 1926).

Ogden, C. K., & Richards, I. A. *The meaning of meaning.* New York: Harcourt Brace & World, 1946. (Originally published, 1923)

Opie I., & Opie, P. *The lore and language of school children.* London: Oxford University Press, 1959.

Osgood, C. E., Suci, G. J., & Tannenbaum, P. H. *The measurement of meaning.* Urbana: University of Illinois Press, 1957.

Peirce, C. S. *The collected papers of Charles Sanders Peirce.* C. Hartshorne & P. Weiss (Eds.) Cambridge: Harvard University Press, 1958.

Peller, L. Language and its prestages. *Bulletin Philadelphia Psychoanalytic Association*, 1964, *14*, 55–76.

Piaget, J. *The psychology of intelligence.* (International Library of Psychology, Philosophy and Scientific Method. London: Routledge & Kegan Paul, 1947.

Piaget, J. (1924) *The language and thought of the child.* Cleveland: World Publishing, 1955.

Piaget, J. *Structuralism.* New York: Basic Books, 1970.

Pine, F. On therapeutic change: Perspectives from a parent-child model. *Psychoanalysis and Contemporary Science*, 1976, *5*, 537–569.

Plato. *The republic.* New York: Basic Books, 1968.

Premack A. J., & Premack, D. Teaching language to an ape. *Scientific American*, 1972, *227*, 92–99.

Premack, D. Language in chimpanzee? *Science*, 1971, *172*, 808–822.

Premack, D. Mechanisms of intelligence: Preconditions for language. In S. R. Harnad, J.

Steklish, & J. Lancaster (Eds.), *Origins and evolution of language and speech* (Vol. 280). New York: Annals of the New York Academy of Sciences, 1976.

Reich, W. The genital character and the neurotic character. In R. Fliess (Ed.), *The psychoanalytic reader*. New York: International Universities Press, 1929.

Reich, W. On character analysis. In R. Fliess (Ed), *The psychoanalytic reader*. New York: International Universities Press, 1948. (Originally published, 1928.)

Ricoeur, P. *Freud and philosophy. An essay on interpretation*. New Haven: Yale University Press, 1970.

Rochester, S. R., Martin, J. R., & Thurston, S. Thought process disorder in schizophrenia: The listener's task. *Brain and Language*, 1977, *4*, 95–114.

Rosen, V. H. The relevance of "style" to certain aspects of defense and the synthetic function of the ego. *International Journal of Psychoanalysis*, 1961, *42*, 447–457.

Rosen, V. H. Disturbances of representation and reference in ego deviations. In R. M. Loewenstein, L. M. Newman, M. Schur, & A. J. Solnit (Eds.), *Psychoanalysis: A general psychology*. New York: International Universities Press, 1966.

Rosen, V. H. The nature of verbal interventions in psychoanalysis. In L. Goldberger & V. Rosen (Eds.), *Psychoanalysis and contemporary science* (Vol. 3). New York: International Universities Press, 1974.

Rosen V. H. *Style, character and language*. M. E. Jucovy & S. Atkin (Eds.), New York: Jason Aronson, 1977.

Rousseau, J.-J. *Emile: Or, education*. New York: E. P. Dutton, 1978. (Originally published, 1761–1762.)

Rubinstein, B. B. On metaphor and related phenomena. *Psychoanalysis and Contemporary Science*, 1972, *1*, 70–108.

Rumbaugh, D. M., & Gill, T. V. The mastery of language-type skills by the chimpanzee (Pan). *Annals of the New York Academy of Sciences*, 1976, *280*, 526–578.

Rumbaugh, D. M., Gill, T. V., & Von Glasersfeld, E. C. Language in man, monkeys, and machines. *Science*, 1974, *185*, 871–873.

Rumbaugh, D. M., Von Glasersfeld, E., Warner, H., Pisani, P., & Gill, T. V. Lana (chimpanzee) learning language: A progress report. *Brain and Language*, 1974, *1*, 205–212.

Rumbaugh, E. S. & Rumbaugh, D. M. Symbolization, language, and chimpanzees: A theoretical reevaluation based on the initial language acquisition processes in four young Pan troglodytes. *Brain and Language*, 1978, *6*, 265–300.

Rumbaugh, E. S., Rumbaugh, D. M., & Boysen, S. Symbolic communications between two chimpanzees. *Science*, 1978, *201*, 641–644.

Russel, B. On denoting. In H. Feigl & W. Sellars (Eds.), *Readings in philosophical analysis*. New York: Appleton-Century-Crofts, 1949.

Salzinger, K., Portnoy, S., & Feldman, R. S. Verbal behavior of schizophrenic and normal subjects. *Annals of the New York Academy of Science*, 1964, *105*, 845–860.

Sander, L. W., Stechler, G., Julia, H., & Burns, P. Primary prevention and some aspects of temporal organization in early infant-caretaker interaction. In E. N. Rexford, L. Sander, & T. Shapiro (Eds.), *Infant psychiatry*. New Haven: Yale University Press, 1976.

Santayana, G. *The life of reason*. New York: Scribner's, 1954.

Sapir, E. *Language: An introduction to the study of speech*. New York: Harcourt, Brace, and World, 1921.

Saussure, de, F. *Course in general linguistics*. New York: Philosophic Library, 1959.

Schachtel, E. *Metamorphosis*. New York: Basic Books, 1959.

Schafer, R. *A new language for psychoanalysis*. New Haven: Yale University Press, 1976.

Schafer, R. *Language and insight*. New Haven: Yale University Press, 1978. (a)

Schafer, R. Conflict as paradoxical actions. *Psychoanalysis and Contemporary Thought*, 1978, *1*, 3–19. (b)

Scheflen, A. E. The significance of posture in communication systems. *Psychiatry*, 1964, 27, 316–331.

Scheflen, A. E. Quasi-courtship behavior in psychotherapy. *Psychiatry*, 1965, 28, 245–257. (a)

Scheflen, A. E. Stream and structure of communicational behavior: Context analysis of a psychotherapy session. Commonwealth of Pennsylvania. EPPI. *Behavioral Studies Monograph*, 1965, No. 1. (b)

Scheflen, A. E. *Communicational structure. Analysis of a psychotherapy transaction.* Bloomington: Indiana University Press, 1973.

Schneirla, T. C. & Rosenblatt, J. S. Behavioral organization and genesis of the social bond in insects and mammals. *American Journal of Orthopsychiatry*, 1961, 31, 223–253.

Searle, J. R. *Speech acts: An essay in the philosophy of language.* New York: Cambridge University Press, 1969.

Searles, H. A. *New perspectives on psychoanalytic therapy with the borderline adult: Some principles concerning technique.* New York: Brunner/Mazel, 1975.

Shapiro, T. Oedipal distortions in severe character pathologies: Developmental and theoretical considerations. *Psychoanalytic Quarterly*, 1977, 66, 559–579. (a)

Shapiro, T. Psychoanalytic research and linguistics. In B. B. Wolman (Ed.), *International Encyclopedia of Psychiatry, Psychology, Psychoanalysis, and Neurology.* New York: Aesculapius, 1977. (b)

Shapiro, T., & Kapit, R. Linguistic negation in autistic and normal children. *Journal of Psycholinguistic Research*, 1978, 7, 337–351.

Shapiro, T., & Perry, R. Latency revisited: The age 7 + − 1. *The Psychoanalytic Study of the Child*, 1976, 31, 79–105.

Shapiro, T., Huebner, H., & Campbell, M. Language behavior and hierarchic integration in a psychotic child. *Journal of Autism and Childhood Schizophrenia*, 1974, 1, 71–90.

Spitz, R. *A genetic field theory of ego formation.* New York: International Universities Press, 1959.

Steingart, I. A comparative psychopathology approach to language behavior. *Communicative Structures and Psychic Structures*, 1977, 1, 175–198.

Steingart, I., & Freedman, N. The organization of body-focused kinesic behavior and language construction in schizophrenic and depressed states. In D. P. Spence (Ed.), *Psychoanalysis and contemporary science* (Vol. 4). New York: International Universities Press, 1975.

Stern, D. A microanalysis of mother-infant interaction. *Journal of the American Academy of Child Psychiatry*, 1971, 10, 501–517.

Stern, D., & Wasserman, G. *The language environment of preverbal infants: Evidence for the central development role of prosodic features.* Unpublished manuscript, 1979.

Stern, D., Jaffe, J., & Beebe, B. Vocalizing in unison and in alternation: Two modes of communication within the mother-infant dyad. *Transactions of the New York Academy of Sciences*, 1975, 263, 89–101.

Stern, W., & Stern, C. *Die Kindersprache.* Leipzig: Barth, 1928.

Stone, L. *The psychoanalytic situation.* New York: International Universities Press, 1961.

Straker, N. *Schematic diagnosing as an aid to the interpretative work with borderline patients.* Unpublished manuscript, 1978.

Sullivan, H. S. *The interpersonal theory of psychiatry.* New York: W. W. Norton, 1953.

Sullivan, H. S. *The psychiatric interview.* New York: W. W. Norton, 1954.

Suomi, S., Harlow, H. F., & McKinney, W. T. Monkey psychiatrists. *American Journal of Psychiatry*, 1972, 128, 927–932.

Szasz, T. S. The problem of psychiatric nosology. *American Journal of Psychiatry*, 1957, 114, 405–413.

Thomas, A., Chess, S., Birch, H. G., Hertzig, M., & Korn, S. *Behavioral individuality in early childhood*. New York: New York University Press, 1963.

Thomas, L. *Lives of a cell: Notes of a biology watcher*. New York: Viking, 1974.

Tobach, E., & Schneirla, T. C. The biopsychology of social behavior in animals. In R. E. Cooke (Ed.), *The biologic basis of pediatric practice*. New York: McGraw-Hill, 1969.

Vygotsky, L. S. *Thought and language*. Cambridge: M.I.T. Press, 1962. (First published, 1934).

Waelder, R. The principle of multiple function. *The Psychoanalytic Quarterly*, 1936, 5, 45–62.

Watson, J. *Psychology from the standpoint of a behaviorist*. Philadelphia: Lippincott, 1919.

Weir, R. *Language in the crib*. The Hague: Mouton, 1964.

Werner, H. *Comparative psychology of mental development*. New York: International Universities Press, 1940.

Werner, H., & Kaplan, B. *Symbol formation*. New York: Wiley, 1963.

Whorf, B. L. *Language, thought, and reality*. Cambridge: M.I.T. Press, 1962.

Wilson, E. Abstract: Revue Française de psychanalyse. *Psychoanalytic Quarterly*, 1978, 47, 151–155.

Wilson, E. *Historicism in psychoanalysis*. Unpublished manuscript, 1978.

Winnicott, D. W. Transitional objects and transitional phenomena: A study of the first not-me possession. *International Journal of Psychoanalysis*, 1953, 34, 89–97.

Winnicott, D. W. *Therapeutic consultations in child psychiatry*. New York: Basic Books, 1971.

Winnicott, D. W. *The piggle*. New York: International Universities Press, 1977.

Wittgenstein, L. *Tractatus logico-philosophicus*. London: Routledge & Kegan Paul, 1951.

Wittgenstein, L. *Philosophical investigations*. New York: Macmillan, 1953.

Wordsworth, W. "My heart leaps up when I behold." In S. F. Gingerich (Ed.), *Selected Poems of William Wordsworth*. Boston: Houghton Mifflin, 1923.

Wortis, J. *Fragments of an analysis with Freud*. New York: Simon & Schuster, 1954.

Index